Mukaka's House

A family's story of God's faithfulness

By Charlie Collins

This book is dedicated to Brandy, Brandon, Cody, Sarah, Isaac, and Faith. Never forget that God will be faithful to you in every step of your life. Keep Him first, and diligently train yourselves to hear His still small voice.

Author: Charlie Collins
Editors: Amy Collins, Brandy Collins, Brandon Collins
Contributors: Amy Collins, Brandon Collins, Jennifer Cromwell, Julie LaPat
Website: www.mukakashouse.com

Published by Charlie and Amy Collins
ISBN-10: 0692401911
ISBN-13: 978-0-692-40191-0

Contents

Chapter 1

Legally Blind

It was a normal Sunday, or so it seemed. I was sitting in our adult Sunday school class when I heard some noise coming from down the hall. I assumed it was some of the youth goofing around and went out to investigate. As I came to the end of the hall and the welcome area of the church, the only person I saw was an elderly man named Bill. Bill was legally blind. He had cataracts that gave him very poor eyesight.

He said, "Charlie is that you?" Surprised that he recognized me, I said, "Yes, it is." He proceeded to tell me that there was a missions trip going to Uganda, Africa and that the team only had women on it. He thought that it would be good if a man were on the team. He asked me if I wanted to go. I thought about it for a second. Actually, I had thought about it for a few years. God had laid Africa on my heart well in advance, but I had no idea of what was to come. My sister, Julie, was the one leading the mission team, but I still thought it was outside the realm of possibilities for me. I told Bill that I wasn't sure if I could make it work. He said, “Listen, Charlie. If you’ll go, I’ll pay your way.” I was in shock. I came out here to send kids back to class and now someone was offering to pay my way to go on a mission trip to Africa!

Julie later said that she had been praying for a man to come with them, and God gave her the biggest guy she knew – her 6’9” tall little brother.

This was the start of a very long and exciting journey to Uganda. It is my prayer that you will see God at work in your life as you read about how He has been continually faithful in ours.

To God be the Glory forever and ever! Amen!

Chapter 2

Comfortable Living

I lived a normal life. Normal in that I had a steady job, a wife, kids, dog, house, and things were going good. We had a comfortable routine. Some may call it a rut, but I think of a rut as a routine you don't like and can't get out of. I enjoyed my life. I enjoyed our garden (as long as I didn't have to weed it), and taking walks with the kids, and having a stay-at-home wife. Sure, there were ups and downs, but all in all I was blessed and content.

Ok. So there's nothing wrong here so far, right? Right. There is nothing wrong with living the life God has given us to live. Worshipping him, loving him, and teaching our kids to do the same. We were active in the church and in the community. We had been involved in a bus ministry at our church, bringing kids and sharing the gospel with them.

We were already doing and going and loving people to Christ. How could it be that God had another plan for us? I don't know the answer to that question. As the weeks and months and years passed, I realized that there's a whole lot that I don't know. But He is faithful. He does have a plan.

His plan included me being on the mission team to Uganda, Africa. This was a plan so life changing that it caused us to give up almost everything comfortable in our lives. This plan was a plan to glorify God and to share His love and grace to people that needed Him. I am so thankful that He included us in His plan.

Chapter 3

Preparation

Uganda is a small country almost in the exact middle of Africa. It has the huge Lake Victoria bordering its East side and is home to the source of the Nile River. It's a beautiful country with lush vegetation and pleasantly warm temperatures since it is located on the equator.

Although English is the national language, many tribal languages are spoken throughout the country even though it is only about the size of the state of Oregon. Colonized by the British in the 1800's, Uganda still has many of the same laws and customs that Great Britain imposed on them during their rule. Since Uganda gained its independence in 1962, there have been many uprisings and conflicts. The most recent one has to do with the Lord's Resistance Army (LRA), which is lead by Joseph Koney.

What greatly disturbed me about Uganda was how the LRA's activities were described in the 2006 documentary film entitled "Invisible Children" ([Invisible Children], 2006. Film). The film documented the LRA's unwavering cruelty towards children and the fear that millions of people felt. In order to gain more soldiers for war, the LRA would ravage villages, setting fire to homes and killing innocent people. They would take the children of the villages and force them to become soldiers – handing them man-sized machine guns and teaching them how to murder. The children who refused would be used as object lessons on how to deaden the senses of those who didn't refuse. Sometimes the children would be forced to murder their own families and then boil them and eat them in order to deaden their consciences.

Thousands upon thousands of children would flee the bush each night and flock to the cities to find refuge. They would sleep in hospital basements, drainage ditches, and fields just to be protected from the LRA. The LRA, though smaller in size, still exists to this day.

As you can imagine, I was more than a little nervous to go on this mission trip. I actually thought I was going to die. I'm not kidding. I knew I was going to be traveling towards the western side of Uganda by myself, which was closer to the LRA's activities. I wrote my wife and kids a final goodbye letter before I left and put it in the safe for them to read in case I did not return.

As the observant reader that you are, you know that I did not die at the hands of the LRA. However, something in me did die. Something so deep that I'm still not sure exactly what it was. What I can say is that I am no longer content in life. I am constantly trying to figure out what God's plan is – where He wants me now. I often feel abnormal, as if there is something wrong with me, but I know that God did not give me this blessing of discontentment without reason. It is for His glory and His honor.

Map of Uganda

Chapter 4

Bakka

It was Sunday, and we were traveling north to a small village called Bakka to worship with a tiny church. The road was bumpy to say the least, and it was hot. Driving in Uganda is an art and a skill that one must learn very quickly when navigating through the winding, rough, and often crowded roads. The driver must be careful to dodge large pot holes, swerve around grazing livestock, avoid people darting across the road at any given time, and somehow manage to miss large buses driving extremely fast on the wrong side of the road. The use of the horn is still somewhat of a mystery to me. They honk the horn and flash their headlights at random times and for what seams like random reasons.

The journey to Bakka, however, was extremely bouncy even for Ugandan standards. Jennifer, a lady on our trip, was sitting in the back of the van. She was getting sick and asked us to pray for her. We prayed, and then I asked if she wanted some motion sickness medicine. To my surprise, she declined and said that she just needed prayer. At that point, I could not understand her perspective. I mean, sure, let's pray about it, but what does it hurt to also take some medicine?

It turns out that it wasn't motion sickness. I learned for the first time, and not the last, that just being in the presence of evil can make you feel sick. See, we had entered into an area of Uganda that practices witchcraft. Jennifer writes it this way in her blog:

> "Unfortunately, on the way there (Bakka) I became unbelievably sick. I was attributing it to motion sickness, which was definitely there. I have never been so car sick in my entire life. I realized I was going downhill quickly, and we had a lengthy drive on a horrendously bumpy dirt road, so I asked for those in the van with me to pray over me. They did and then Stephanie (one of the missionaries) told me that she experiences sickness every time that she enters certain areas in Uganda. She went on to tell us about the spiritual background of the area. Witchcraft, human sacrifices, and demons were all prevalent in this area. The church we were visiting bought property where the demonic presence was the most powerful. Basically, we were going into a spiritual war zone. Stephanie encouraged me to just pray in the Spirit for a release from the oppression that was taking hold of my body. Once we drove onto the church property I felt great. God showed up!!!"

I was completely ignorant to all of this at this point in the journey. I was just sitting in the front seat of the van looking around and noticing things like 8-foot tall termite mounds and skinny cows with oversized horns. Things weren't strange to me until right when we pulled into the church property. In order to get to the church, we had to pass under an enormous tree. The trunk of the tree had a diameter of approximately 8 to 10 feet. The roots of the tree weren't just under the ground. Large swaths of them sprawled out across the entrance to the property. We actually had to drive over and through the roots to get to the church.

As I unfolded my 6'9" body out of the tiny vehicle, I started towards my sister, Julie, who had been riding in a different van with another missionary named Randy. Randy was basically a walking Uganda encyclopedia. He prided himself on being a student of Ugandan culture and their ways of life. He was the type of guy that if you needed something, Randy knew who to talk to, where to get it, how to get there, and how much it would cost in both shillings and dollars. So as you might expect, Julie was getting quite the history lesson in the other van on the way to Bakka. As I approached her at the church, she said to me, "Did you hear about this area?" Clueless in so many ways, I said, "No. What about it?" She proceeded to tell me.

(The tree in front of the church at Bakka)
Photo taken by Julie LaPat

After Julie told me about the background of the area, I felt my stomach drop and felt a sadness that I cannot fully explain. By this point, the church service had already started. We were quickly ushered into the front of the church and sat down in the "pews" or wooden benches with no backs. Like so much of this mission trip, I did not have time to mentally process what was going on.

During the first part of the service, Pastor Fred told us about some of the history of the church. The property was purchased from a local witch doctor. Then they built the church on the property. It was a simple building made of wood and sheet metal.

(Woman reading Bible in Bakka church)
Photo taken by Julie LaPat

After a while, the church building started to lean. This doesn't mean much to you and I, but to them, in the environment they were in, this was a big deal.

Satan worshippers started to say that the devil was tearing down their church. Many in the church became frightened. The Pastor before Fred and many of the congregation fled.

The church members then decided to build a new building. It was made of stronger materials. Just a week before we arrived, they had poured a cement floor. The worship that day was to be remembered! There was dancing, singing, rejoicing, drumming, yelling, and praising God. See, a cement floor means less dirt and dust to you and I. But to this church experiencing immense persecution, a cement floor meant stability and strength.

Pastor Fred went on to explain more about the giant tree at the entrance of the property. He said that satan worshippers all around the area believe that demons live in that tree and play drums in it at night. That tree is the main focal point for the witchcraft in that area and it sits on the church property! Pastor Fred wants to cut down that tree. I can only imagine what might happen if he did.

As a courtesy, the host church will normally ask their guests to give them a word from God. While Pastor Fred was giving his introduction, I felt God telling me that I would be the first to speak. At that very moment, Pastor Fred looked directly at me and invited me up to speak. I was stunned. This is what I wrote in my blog later on:

"In Uganda, if a person's hand is dirty, they will not hold out there hand to greet you. They will hold out their wrist or forearm to show that they are unclean. God laid this on my heart to share in relation to His love. He laid this on my heart before I knew that we were going to be speaking in a service. Once we arrived at the church, Julie told me the history of the area and how they still sacrifice children on a mountain nearby. An overwhelming rush of sadness struck me.

Toward the middle of the service, Pastor Fred asked if someone wanted to give their testimony. I really felt like I needed to talk first, but I wondered if someone in the congregation was going to speak first and then allow the visitors to speak. The pastor then looked right at me and said for me to come up. I did. I was so nervous. I wasn't necessarily nervous about speaking in front of people, but I was nervous because God had just spoken to me. I later wondered if the guy on our team behind me had raised his hand to speak, and I just jumped in his spot, but he said that he didn't.

I went on to talk about how we can't hold our hand out to greet God. We need to use our wrist because our spirit is dirty with sin. But God doesn't come to shake our hand, He comes to clean it. As I started to talk about the satanic worship and specifically the human sacrifices, I choked up and had to stop. I told them that I too was a human sacrificer. I too was a human mutilator. It was my sin that drove the nails into Jesus's hands. It was my sin that hoisted Him up on that cross. It was my sin that pierced his body to drain the fluid. It was my sin that sent Him to the grave.

It was by God's power that He rose and conquered my sin."

I cannot tell you fully how much the Holy Spirit moved in that place throughout that service. The Ugandan choir started praising and dancing, and I longed to jump on stage with them! Afterwards, I was talking to Stella, our interpreter from Uganda. I told her how I wanted to dance. She asked me why I didn't. I explained that I'm white, and white people normally don't dance in church (or at least the churches I've been accustomed to). I told her that we may be standing still on the outside, but we are dancing on the inside. She said something I will never forget. She said, "We are sometimes dancing on the outside, but standing still on the inside." What she was essentially saying to me was that it is less about how you worship God, and more that you are truly worshipping God.

Before we started on the long and bumpy journey to our next destination, I took a bottle of water and walked towards the giant tree at the entrance to the church. I prayed a prayer over the water and started pouring the water out around the bottom of the tree as

I hiked all the way around the large roots. I prayed that God would make the water living water and that people in that village would come to know Him.

As we were driving over the bumpy roots to leave, I told the missionary, "I wonder how long Pastor Fred has to live."

Chapter 5

The Prison

We were on the road again, but this time we were going with Bethel church to Sentema Prison to minister to the inmates. Once again, the roads were extremely bumpy, but I somehow managed to fall asleep. This is surprising considering I had a hard time sleeping on the plane on the way to Uganda. When I woke up, we were approaching the prison. The drive up to the prison was surrounded by well-kept green grass. There were prisoners coming out of the prison with jerry cans (water jugs) to fetch water.

We came up to the entrance of the prison and went through the front gate and were greeted by a woman guard, who confiscated our cell phones and nothing else. I'm still not fully sure of the purpose of it. Like so many other things, we just accepted it and moved through the second gate into the prison courtyard.

The courtyard was surrounded by an 8-foot tall fence with barbed wire on the top. Behind us was the entrance to the prison, and in front of us was what

(Sentema Prison)
Photo taken by Julie LaPat

looked like the prison barracks. Julie described it like this:

> "Imagine this: beautiful land. Grass growing outside. 8 ft walls. Prisoners walking around outside the walls going to and from getting water. When entering, you must give them (the lady at the front desk) your cell phone. You can take a bag, or whatever else you want inside. We took in a huge bag of bread, a box full of soap, and feminine hygiene products. After entering the front door, you go through 1-gated door (not even sure if it was locked). You then enter into a courtyard. Across the courtyard are the wards. They are in 1 building. 6 rooms. Each

> room is 16ft x 16ft. Each room has no furniture, no beds, nothing. 28 men share each room. On the porch of this ward were sitting the inmates in their bright yellow uniforms (which they just got recently, before that they had no clothes). The men were sitting perfectly still. The women (about 10) were on the side of the building sitting on the grass."

There was about 50 of us there ministering to the prisoners. Along side of us was the warden. He stood about 5'7" tall and probably only weighed about 140 pounds. He was carrying a machine gun. It was hot and dry, and there wasn't much wind. Here we were, in Uganda Africa, standing inside a prison with about 200 prisoners facing us.

We started singing and worshipping. Bethel church sang a song and then the Mzungus, or white people, sang another song – "Open the Eyes of My Heart, Lord." God did exactly that.

And then, caught by surprise, they asked me to speak. Just before I started walking up there, one of the missionaries told me, "Don't give the salvation message. We will do that at the end." Like so many things on this mission, I can't fully explain the feeling I had at that moment. I am positive that the Holy Spirit took over me as I gave the message in those next minutes.

Before going on the mission to Uganda, I had been involved in a basketball ministry at our church. At first, it was just some guys playing pick up games, but then more and more people started coming. Then, Billy Graham came to town and a group of us went to the "Leadership Training." We thought to ourselves, why aren't we doing this type of evangelism when we play basketball? We started to give lessons and present the gospel of Jesus Christ, and many men, women, and children accepted Christ as their Lord and Savior – Big Jesus!!!

As I stood there before the group of African men, it reminded me of being in front of the men in the basketball gym when I would give the devotion. I told the prisoners about the basketball ministry and about Jesus Christ and about His love for them. I told them how I would present this message to the men at the basketball ministry and that there were two guys who would always sit in the back, as some of the men were doing at the prison. These two guys would talk and joke and play on their phones. They would cause trouble and even get into fights. One night they even bashed windows in the parking lot. But each Wednesday night they heard the Gospel message and refused to accept it.

I told the prisoners that one night, one of the basketball players named Korrus Harrison and his friend went to a party at Oklahoma State University. They were denied entry and got upset. They went and got a gun and started shooting at the people at the party – killing one and wounding others.

Korrus mailed me a letter from jail, asking me to be a character witness for him at the court trial. I said that I would but that I would have to tell the truth. I would have to say that he was disrespectful, that he got into fights, and that he bashed in windows. I told Korrus that some day he is going to have another trial in front of God. He is going to need a lot more than a character witness. Jesus offers to be more than a character witness. He offers to take our punishment for us so that we may be with Him forever.

I told the Ugandan prisoners that they also have a choice to make. They can sit back and listen and reject the gift that God has offered them like Korrus did, or they can accept this free gift and live for Jesus.

I write in my blog: "They were told that they may have to be kept inside the prison walls, but that it's their choice if they want to break free from the chains that bind their souls. It was awesome to hear their shouts of joy! Praise Jesus!"

I asked them who wants to accept Christ into their heart and hands went up everywhere. I was in shock. Only by the grace and power of God did I get through the salvation prayer.

Julie writes: "180 of the 200 people accepted Jesus into their heart!!!!! Talk about a revival in that prison!!!"

As I walked back to my team, I looked over and tears were streaming down their faces. The Holy Spirit moved in a way I had never experienced. This might sound odd, but the best way to explain how that moment felt was captured in the movie, "The Passion of the Christ." ([Icon Productions], 2004. Film.) The men were about to stone the adulterous woman, and Jesus just started writing in the dirt. It was a hot sunny day, and Jesus was writing in slow motion with every sound audible as His finger was breaking through the fragile earth's crust. In some ways, that is how that moment felt to me. So powerful and real, it was a moment that will be added to my testimony the rest of the days of my life.

After I spoke, Josh went up to speak. Josh was a young man in his early twenties and was fun to be around. He had come to live in Uganda with his parents for a short while, and all of the Ugandan kids loved him. Josh spoke about how Jesus is the bread of life. As I listened to him, I wondered, "How are they going to eat the bread of life without the word of God?" I then prayed that God would reveal the right person to be given my Bible. There was a man that was obviously deeply moved in the Spirit, and I knew that he was the one. Then, ashamedly, I started to worry and be afraid. I would love to leave this part out, but I can't. I started going through my Bible, taking out anything that had my personal information on it. Oh how I wish this were the only thing I had to be ashamed of on this day. I will tell you more about that later.

After Josh was done speaking, everyone was still and quiet. I walked up to the warden in full view of everyone and asked him if I could give someone my Bible. He said, "Yes." I proceeded over to the young man. He had his head down and didn't see me coming. I placed my hand on his shoulder, and he looked up at me with tears in his eyes. I handed him my Bible, and then something completely unexpected happened. The prisoners started clapping. Who knew the massive amount of joy that could come from inside a prison's walls? This can only come from Jesus.

It was awesome to see God touching the hearts of so many people, but at the same time, I was feeling anxious to leave. However, we had one more thing to do. The group from Bethel had brought a giant bag of bread and other items to give to the prisoners. The prisoners were used to this and were starting to come forward and squat down on the ground in four separate lines. Most of the mission team was starting to leave, but the group from Bethel needed help passing out the bread.

My sister came up to me and said that she was going to stay and help. She thought I should too. Every part of my being did not want to stay and help, but since Julie was going to stay, I did not want to leave her in there alone. This is what I wrote:

> "As most of the people left the prison, Julie stayed behind to hand out the bread to the prisoners. I would've rather left and let someone else pass it out, but since my sister stayed behind I didn't want to leave her. All of the men lined up, squatting on the ground. As we handed out three pieces of bread to each, they would hide it anywhere on their body so that they could get another three pieces. They were starving.
>
> I got a little nervous when it came down to the end because I wondered if there would be enough. We let the men hand out the rest of the bread, and Julie and I left. I didn't want to be caught with my sister in the middle of upset people if there wasn't enough bread. God has protected us this entire trip and allowed us to be a part of and see miracles. Why was I so scared about handing out bread? Jesus is the bread of life! My faith was lacking in the midst of uncertainty."

Julie writes:

> "It was very humbling today. God loves these prisoners just as much as He loves you and me. He died for these prisoners, just as He died for

you and me! It was a privilege to serve God today."

Matthew 25:35-46:

"For I was hungry and you gave me something to eat, I was thirsty and you gave me something to drink, I was a stranger and you invited me in, I needed clothes and you clothed me, I was sick and you looked after me, I was in prison and you came to visit me.' "Then the righteous will answer him, 'Lord, when did we see you hungry and feed you, or thirsty and give you something to drink? When did we see you a stranger and invite you in, or needing clothes and clothe you? When did we see you sick or in prison and go to visit you?' "The King will reply, 'Truly I tell you, whatever you did for one of the least of these brothers and sisters of mine, you did for me.'

"Then he will say to those on his left, 'Depart from me, you who are cursed, into the eternal fire prepared for the devil and his angels. For I was hungry and you gave me nothing to eat, I was thirsty and you gave me nothing to drink, I was a stranger and you did not invite me in, I needed clothes and you did not clothe me, I was sick and in prison and you did not look after me.' "They also will answer, 'Lord, when did we see you hungry or thirsty or a stranger or needing clothes or sick or in prison, and did not

> help you?' "He will reply, 'Truly I tell you, whatever you did not do for one of the least of these, you did not do for me.' "Then they will go away to eternal punishment, but the righteous to eternal life."

Of course, there was enough bread for all of the prisoners. If Jesus can feed 5,000 with one loaf, He can feed 200 with a garbage sack full of bread.

Chapter 6

The Hospital

We pulled up to a Ugandan hospital in a people mover type of bus. Randy's wife, Alisa, stood up in front of the bus to prepare us for what was about to happen. She said that we should expect God to work miracles as we pray for the sick. After all that had happened on this mission, I was expecting miracles. She went on to say that the patients expect to be healed.

The hospital was nothing like a hospital in the United States. It consisted of a few one-story buildings tied together by sidewalks. There was a men's ward, a women's ward, and a children's ward. I went into the men's ward to pray with the men.

The men's ward was a spacious open room with old hospital beds in rows. It reminded me of the infirmaries in old war movies – no privacy and everyone could be seen. The hospital staff is not responsible for the daily care of the patient. The patient must have a relative or friend come and help with changing the sheets as well as feeding and bathing him or her. It is a major financial undertaking to be in the hospital and an extreme burden on the family.

Like usual, it was hot. However, in the hospital it was hot, and there wasn't much air movement. Add to the stale atmosphere a pungent odor mixed with unpleasant sights, and conditions were ripe for feeling very uncomfortable.

Steve was one of the missionaries with me inside the men's ward. Steve and his wife Stephanie are from Oklahoma, and they are how Julie found out about the missions trip. Steve is a guy that loves to crack jokes and puns even if he is the only one who laughs at them. He can lighten an uncomfortable situation just by his personality and calm demeanor. His love for Uganda's people is to be admired. Once a pastor in Oklahoma, God called him to Uganda, and he obeyed.

Having Steve in the hospital room to lead and guide us was very comforting to say the least. We walked from bedside to bedside and prayed with the men. It was the kind of prayer that was extremely powerful and Spirit filled. I can say that I had never experienced prayer like that before. Strangely, it was completely exhausting. We had prayed for almost everybody in the room, and I told Steve, "I have to leave, I don't feel good." I went outside. I stood under an awning in the fresh air for a few minutes, trying to regain my strength.

After a while, Steve came outside. I told him, "I'm sorry I had to leave, but I felt exhausted and sick." Steve reassured me that it is normal in those situations to sometimes have that reaction. Prayer can take a lot of energy sometimes. Thinking about the scripture, it reminds me of the time that the sick lady touched Jesus's robe:

> "And a woman was there who had been subject to bleeding for twelve years, but no one could heal her. She came up behind him and touched the edge of his cloak, and immediately her bleeding stopped.
>
> 'Who touched me?' Jesus asked.
>
> When they all denied it, Peter said, 'Master, the people are crowding and pressing against you.'
>
> But Jesus said, 'Someone touched me; I know that power has gone out from me.'
>
> Then the woman, seeing that she could not go unnoticed, came trembling and fell at his feet. In the presence of all the people, she told why she had touched him and how she had been instantly healed. Then he said to her, 'Daughter, your faith has healed you. Go in peace.' Luke 8:43

Jesus knew that someone had touched Him because He could feel the power going out from Him. If He could detect that power left Him, how much more weak would I be after praying for healing?

As powerful as the prayer time was in the men's ward, the women were also experiencing the Holy Spirit's healing power as well. This is what my sister writes:

> "We left Jinja today and went to go pray at a hospital. It is not like a hospital in America. This hospital has different wards. The ward that (the women) went into was the Maternity ward...
>
> The first eight women we prayed for had had c-sections. Some of them were Christians and some Muslims. Two ladies we prayed for were partially through their pregnancies and had malaria. It is really bad to be pregnant and have malaria and is really bad for the baby. So, the mothers are in the hospital until they are no longer with fever. One of the ladies was a born-again (Christian), and one a Muslim. Each of them allowed us to pray for them. The Muslim girl was wet with sweat when we finished. When we were done praying for the other women in the ward, we looked over and the Muslim girl had packed her bags and was going home! SHE WAS HEALED!!! ... She was laughing and smiling. We told her that God healed her! She was happy! We were happy!!!

(Woman rejoicing after being healed
by the power of the Holy Spirit!)
Photo taken by Julie LaPat

The other lady with malaria was not in her bed either!

Two of the women had delivered their babies stillborn. It was really tough. I could tell that we were providing comfort to those ladies. Two of us had had children who had died. We were able to understand, and let them know that.

One of the ladies we prayed for had been in the hospital in labor (with mild labor pains) for a week. She was due. She needed prayer to go into labor with hard labor pains. We prayed for her to begin to have full labor pains. By the time we were done praying for the other women, she was kneeling on the floor outside the delivery room waiting to deliver her baby. She was in active full on labor! What a miracle!! …

As sad, and as uncomfortable that some/all of us were today, we know without a doubt that God used us today. I am honored to be used by God today. I know that God will use us everyday, we just have to allow Him to work through us. We need to expect miracles! Expect healing! It happens!"

Once we returned from Uganda, many people wanted to hear about our experiences. One of the most often asked questions was, "Why doesn't God heal people in America like He did on your mission trip?" Wow! What a tough question! It is a tough question because it begs the recipient of the question to be tempted to try to pry open the mind of God. I cannot pretend to know why God does what He does. What I can say is that the people believed that they would be healed, and God healed them. The question could also be answered with another question, "Why do you believe that He doesn't?"

"But I will restore you to health
and heal your wounds,
declares the Lord,
'because you are called an outcast,
Zion for whom no one cares.'"
Jeremiah 30:17

Chapter 7

Mbarara

It was time for me to brave Uganda on my own. I was off to visit a Compassion International child named Arinanye, that we had been sponsoring for about ten years. She lived in western Uganda around the city of Mbarara, which was about six hours away from Kampala. It was early in the morning, approximately 5:30 am, and I was heading out of the hotel and down the stairs to the stone paved parking lot. The parking lot was enclosed by a tall fence with barbed wire on top and a huge metal gate. To the side of the parking lot is the kitchen area, and the main chef came out to greet me. "Would you like something to eat before you go?" he asked. I declined but said that I would like a glass of orange juice. I was so nervous I couldn't eat. Actually, I was scared. I thought that this was the point in the trip that I was going to die.

That sounds ridiculous as I type it out, but it is true. I had heard about the Lord's Resistance Army and the destruction that they caused and was fearful for my own safety. I was traveling alone with a taxi driver whom I had never met. I would have no idea if he were taking me in the right direction or not. My fear was so strong that I had actually written a letter to my wife and kids in case I didn't return and put it in our safe at home before I left.

At that moment, at the peak of my fear, Jennifer opened her hotel room window on the second floor and said, "Charlie, I am praying for you." I cannot express the relief that swept over me just from those few words. It was like God was telling me, "You are going to be OK." It's amazing what the power of words and prayer can do!

My taxi van came, and the driver and I headed west towards Mbarara. Before we even left Kampala, the capital city of Uganda, I looked down, and my phone battery had died. I had plugged it into the charger the night before, but the maid had come in and turned off all of the outlets to save electricity! Even though I should have been panicked, I had a peace about it all. God was answering Jennifer's prayer at that moment.

About 45 minutes into the trip, I realized that I should not have drunk so much orange juice. There are very few places to stop between Kampala and Mbarara in case you were wondering. But, when in Uganda do like Ugandans. After providing nourishment to the surrounding shrubs, we were back on the road.

The drive was amazing and the country is really beautiful. There are hills and mountains with trees and banana plantations all over. People are pushing bikes loaded down with bananas. The roads, for the most part, are pretty bad. There is a long stretch that is good, but many of them are under construction. I figured out that if I sat in the middle of the van instead of the front seat that I didn't bump as hard.

As we pulled up to the Compassion International compound, I couldn't help but notice the fields of banana trees and coffee plantations. It was absolutely gorgeous. They had a simple office building, playground, school building, and even a church on the grounds. The office area had a large entry set up with a couple tables. One table had local delicacies to eat. They had done all of this for me! I was overwhelmed with the hospitality that they showed me. Then they pulled out the grade sheets of Arinanye, our sponsored child, and explained how she was doing in school.

We then left and went to find Arinanye – which proved to be a difficult task. She had activities that she was involved in, and they had a hard time finding her. We eventually went to her house and met with her grandparents and cousins. Her parents are dead, so she lives with her grandma. Five out of twelve of the grandma's kids have died due mainly to illnesses. Arinanye finally arrived, and it was very special to see her in person. We exchanged greetings and presents and sat down to eat a small snack.

In Uganda, it is rude to go to somebody's house and not partake of the food they put before you. Arinanye's grandparents had put out small bananas and a warm coke. I knew that this was very generous for them since a coke is somewhat expensive to buy. However, I had just eaten at the Compassion compound and was not feeling like I could eat much. It was warm inside the house, and it had a strange odor. I can't eat much when I'm nervous, and this was one of those times. I managed to drink a little bit of warm coke, but the fact that I didn't eat did not go unnoticed. My interpreter had to explain to them that I had just eaten.

The grandmother then went on in our conversation to say that she wanted us to pray for her husband who had never accepted Jesus as his Savior. As I think back about that experience, it makes me think of me rejecting their food and how that must have made them feel. I wish I would have taken at least one bite so as not to offend them. But then I think about Arinanye's grandfather and what God has offered him.

God has set before him a table of forgiveness, a son He sacrificed, grace that we could never earn, eternal salvation, blessings, and a relationship with God Himself. When he chooses to reject the gifts of nourishment from God, her grandpa is rejecting Him. Sometimes I wonder if I would have just explained the gospel in that context if her grandfather would have understood.

Chapter 8

God Bless the USA

As we continued on our journey in Uganda, we went to a beautiful area around Jinja. I didn't realize that what I was about to experience would make me see the USA in a whole new light. This is what I wrote that night:

"Tonight, we were at the Nile River and enjoyed a boat ride, and then went to the white water rapid area. It was beautiful. Yale University students were there, and one student, who was from Kampala I believe, fell into the river and most likely died. One or two of our team members saw an arm raised and then go under. As tragic as this was for everyone, it wasn't as depressing as the guys that had the boats. They said that they would go look if they were paid. Once paid, they asked for more money. After a while, they finally went out and looked. I heard that the police said that this happened before, and they hid the body until they were paid even more. I've had a hard time tonight trying to wrap my brain around it all.

Before you go to bed tonight, please pray with your families. Thank God that we live in a country that values each person. Thank God that we live in a country that total strangers will help out someone in need because it's the right thing to do. Thank God that we live in a country that will send aid to other countries in need. Thank God that we live in a country where parents still teach their kids the difference between right and wrong according to the Holy Bible. Thank God that He has not turned His back on us even though we deserve it as a nation. I don't know how many times I've thought that I am so blessed to live in the USA. We are blessed no matter how much credit card debt is piled up!!! We are blessed no matter how many hours a week we work!!! (They go home on the weekends to see their families). We are blessed no matter who is president or which political party is in power! We are blessed no matter what the stock market says! We are blessed! We are blessed, America!

After all of that, we went to a different hotel to stay the night. There was about five or six police there to go through our bags and scan our bodies as if we were going on an airplane. This is at a hotel. What am I going to do, shoot someone because they didn't scramble my eggs in the morning? My question is that about a mile away someone died in the Nile River. Where were the police then?

God bless the USA. God bless Uganda."

What I didn't write in my blog was how God protected me from something that day. I'm not even exactly sure what it was. We were at Bujugali Falls enjoying the sights. It's a modest waterfall with giant rocks protruding out into the river. There was a young crippled Ugandan man with a pole about 10 feet long. He would climb this pole and bounce it around so that he could balance. It was an amazing sight to see. There he was, a crippled man about nine feet in the air jumping around on a pole. If you are asking yourself, "Why would he do that?" you were reading my mind. But Ugandans are clever opportunists. While he was doing that, there was another man going around collecting money for him. If you were enjoying the show, you were expected to pay up. I didn't enjoy the show that much.

There were also guys there with "jerry cans", which are yellow jugs used to carry water. I would guess that they could hold about five gallons of water at a time. These guys had empty jerry cans and, if you paid them money, they would go to the top of the waterfall and ride the jerry cans down it. Like I said, it was a modest waterfall, but it was still amusing to watch. Ugandans might find it even more amusing because most Ugandans cannot swim.

(Crippled man jumping on pole for money)
Photo taken by Julie LaPat

At one point I decided to walk out on a large rock protruding into the falls. It was about four feet wide, and I felt safe. However, one of the bigger guys collecting money for the "shows" came up behind me, blocking me in. He had his hand out asking for money. I said no, and he didn't move. He asked for money again. I said in Luganda, "Muveo!" which means "Move!", and he moved out of the way.

At this point, I decided I just wanted some time alone and told Steve, one of the missionaries, that I was going to hike up the hill. I hiked up and found a swing set with a large bench type swing and sat there. Some local kids came up to me, and we watched the monkeys in the trees, ate sweetarts®, and did our best to talk to each other. Before I knew it, an entire hour had passed by. I wondered what everybody was doing, so I started to head back down the hill.

As I approached the bottom of the hill, Julie came out to meet me with a worried look on her face. She said that she was worried about me since she hadn't seen me in a while. She told me about the young Ugandan man named Donovan who was with the group from Yale that had fallen in the rapids. I was heartbroken. I went out to the edge of the rocks just looking around as if there was something I could do about it. After a little while, we all left. What an empty feeling it was to just turn around and leave.

We went up to the top of a Bujugali Falls lookout and ate dinner at a "Mexican" restaurant. It was a very solemn atmosphere. Some of my team had just witnessed a death, and now we were going on with life as if it didn't happen. I couldn't help but wonder why God had taken me completely out of that situation. I still wonder about that to this day. What was it that He protected me from? Why did I need to leave? Did it have to do with my feeling of dying in Uganda before I left home?

Randy got a call the next day that said they found Donovan's body on the bank of the Nile River.

(Local men searching for Donovan at Bujugali Falls)
Photo taken by Julie LaPat

Chapter 9

VBS in Kalit

We were driving to a small village named Kalit, and I was riding with Steve. He pulled over, and to the girls' dismay, asked me if I wanted to drive. Here we were in a third world country, where the roads are horrendous, motorcycles were whizzing in and out, potholes everywhere, and where driving is on the opposite side of the road, and Steve wanted to know if I wanted to drive? Of course I did! I think the girls were a little bit unnerved that I was behind the wheel. I have to say that I did pretty well if you don't count that one near miss with an oncoming car. It was probably just a coincidence that Steve never asked if I wanted to drive again.

So we pulled up to this tiny church building, and it reminded me a lot of the church we went to in Bakka. As a matter of fact, Kalit isn't too far away from Bakka. There is witchcraft in this area as well, and about half of the population is Muslim. We were going to have a VBS session with all of the kids in the area and thought that there might be around 100 kids attending. God brought double that! Check out what I wrote:

"Today we went to a church building outside of town. The building was really just brick walls and a roof and some uneven concrete, but it did the job nicely. On the way there, I felt a bit queasy, and when we got there, I felt sick head on. I couldn't do my part of the VBS skit and really wanted to go back to the hotel. While I prayed and then Randy prayed, I could feel God helping me feel better. After truth or dare with the African john, I was ready to go. I never remember feeling that sick and then feeling completely better in such a short time before. I really believe the devil wanted me gone because after I felt better there was a little bit of lag time, and I presented the gospel to the kids. Many of them came to Christ. Many of the kids were Muslim. Praise God!

Another precious story from today happened when we were starting VBS. There was a little girl who wouldn't come within 100 feet of us strange white people. We would wave, and she would step back. I walked a little towards her, and she took off running. I thought it was so funny. She really wanted to be in the church but was scared. I threw her some sweetarts® (they love sweetarts®), and she started eating them. A little later I held up a piece of gum. She yelled at me in her native language (and I understood) to throw it to her. I shook my head "no". I put it on a brick on the church wall. Over the next 30 minutes, she literally inched closer and closer to the gum. She eventually came inside the church!!!"

(Children raising their hand to accept Jesus as their Savior)
Photo taken by Julie LaPat

As I think back about this experience, I am reminded of the devil's schemes. He will do almost anything to keep Jesus out of our lives and the lives around us. He will use sickness, discouragement, pride, fear, jealousy, and the lack of faith to keep us down. I can see the effects of his schemes in my life from time to time. Sometimes I get discouraged and don't want to be involved in ministry on a particular day. Sometimes my wife and I will get into an argument just at the "right" time as to make us not want to pray together before bedtime. This story is a good reminder for us to take note of the devil's schemes and to use the power of prayer to fight through those times and let the Holy Spirit breathe new life into us.

Chapter 10

Giving

When it rains in Uganda, it usually pours. The dirt there reminds me of Oklahoma red clay dirt. When it rains, it gets slippery and slimy and gets on everything and is hard to clean. This was one of those days. This is what I wrote:

> "There was so much mud and muck out on the road today that it was hard to get over the "ew" feeling. Not just on the road, everywhere. In the buildings, scraped on the stairs, in the cars, everywhere. Had we just stayed inside, we would've missed out on what God had in store for us. I'm sure the girls will follow up with more of that but it was awesome. We met our youth group's compassion child. We were reserved the front row seat at the "wash your hands" performance at the orphanage. We even danced up on stage with the band members! The mamas (women to care for the children) and teachers even got up there. They said, "That never happens!" We've heard that a lot since we've been here.

When we first arrived in Uganda, we were told not to give out anything (money, clothes, candy, etc.) because the kids shouldn't look to white people as their savior but only to Jesus. This is the muddy part of this trip to me. People here know that white people from the USA are rich (and we all are... believe me). I never want someone to believe that I am his or her savior. But is that a good reason to not give? At what point am I labeled the greedy white Christian? Wasn't it Paul who performed miracles in Lystra and was worshiped? Didn't he correct them? Did he not keep performing miracles in Jesus name? Why then should we worry about giving the gifts God gave to us?

This is my struggle. This is what I wrestle with while I am in Uganda. I know there are good reasons not to give. I know there are good reasons to give.

Please pray for me."

This is a struggle that I continue to wrestle with to this day. I think everybody struggles with it to some degree. When do we give and to whom do we give? I think the answer to that question is more about listening than it is giving. When we are in a right relationship with God, we can hear what He is telling us to do. When we can hear Him, we can obey His instructions.

For example, I was walking down the sidewalk in Kampala, Uganda and there was a little child, no more than 18 months old, sitting up with his legs crossed and his hands cupped in his lap, begging for money. I was stunned. Nobody was around him. He was all alone… or so it seemed. I walked a little further and about 20 feet away was another child in the same position. And then there was another child and then another. I looked all around me for somebody looking out for these children. Out in the middle of the busy road, on the median, were about four ladies looking at their children. They had placed them on the sidewalk and were waiting for people to give them money.

This was sickening to me. I wouldn't have even thought to give them any money. They were using their little kids as pawns to make a living, and it made me angry. It was an easy decision for me to walk on by because I could see right through their plot.

On the other hand, I was walking down a different road in Kampala some time later. A crippled man was sitting on the sidewalk. It wasn't as busy of a road, but I knew he couldn't have gotten there on his own. Someone must have carried him there and placed him on the sidewalk. Begging was his daily job. I knew that the person that carried him would probably be getting a cut of the earnings, so once again I just walked on by. I walked about 15 feet, and God told me to go back and give this man some money. I did.

I learned that the difference between when to give and when not to give someone a donation relies on the logic that God has given to each of us, but it also relies on God – who defies our logic sometimes. I wish I could say that in each instance of giving and not giving I did exactly what God wanted me to do, but I can't. There were times on the mission trip that I gave when I shouldn't and times that I didn't give when I should have.

It is good to wrestle with the fact that helping can hurt, but it is also good to keep in mind, as this verse from James points out, that not helping can hurt too.

> "Suppose a brother or a sister is without clothes and daily food. If one of you says to them, 'Go in peace; keep warm and well fed,' but does nothing about their physical needs, what good is it?" James 2:15-16

Chapter 11

Hope

We spent a lot of time at Hope Children's Home during our mission in Uganda. Hope wasn't far from our hotel, and sometimes we even walked there. From our hotel, we walked down into a valley and then back up the hill along some dirt roads and by houses made of brick and sheet metal. Down in the valley, there was a creek, some stagnant pools of water, and a trash dump – or latrine as they call it. We often saw children playing in the water, trying to catch little fish with their shirts, or they might be picking through the garbage, trying to salvage some food.

Most days we drove to Hope along the dirty, dusty, and very bumpy roads. It sits on maybe two acres of land and consists of a few dormitories, a church, schoolrooms, storage rooms, bathrooms, and a Ugandan kitchen. As we drove up to the gate, the security guard came and opened it for us. We had entered paradise. Not like the paradise you and I would expect. However, the children in the area that are not fortunate enough to live at Hope, call it "paradise."

Children would come from everywhere, running up to the van and waiting for us to open our doors. Once we did, it was a free for all. They grabbed our hands, checked out our pockets, examined our backpacks, and pinched our white skin.

We played with the children, read them stories, told about Jesus, and showed them Christ's love. Over the next two weeks, everyone on our team fell in love with these kids. We listened to their stories and how they ended up at Hope.

One of the kids, I will call him Paul, was from an area that was heavy into witchcraft and child sacrifice. There were men that would go around looking for children to sacrifice. Parents were often scared for the lives of their children. Some would even cut a notch out of their son or daughter's ear so that the witch doctor would not sacrifice them since they were blemished. There was a demand for child sacrifices, as some businessmen believed that having a child sacrificed and then buried underneath their business was good luck.

Paul was living in one of those areas and found himself being hunted by men trying to capture him to be used as a child sacrifice. He was running from the men and decided to veer off the path and hide in the bush. As he lay there as quiet as he could be, he heard the men approaching. He then looked over and there, lying right beside him, was a poisonous snake. Paul knew that if he moved away from the snake that the men would spot him and capture him but that if he stayed still, the snake might strike him. He prayed in that moment that God would rescue him from the snake and the evil men. Miraculously, God answered his prayer. Can you imagine the fear that must have been racing through this little boy's veins? He was eventually taken to Hope and has been there ever since.

Another little boy, named Edward, was brought to Hope by some church members. Edward's mom was lame and unable to walk. She couldn't provide the essentials for Edward, and he was eventually taken to his father for care. His father disowned Edward and threw him into the garbage heap. Some neighbors heard him crying and took him to the church.

A young girl named Prossy was brought to Hope after her parents died. Her extended family was caught trying to sell her as a slave.

There was another young boy named Tony who lost his mom. His father remarried but Tony's step-mom abused him and whipped him with wires. His father only came home on the weekends due to his work, and Tony only got to eat when his father was home.

Juliet also lost her parents due to illness. They most likely died from AIDS. They lived deep in the village where her mother had been a maid for an elderly couple. That couple was unable to properly care for Juliet, so they brought her to Hope.

These are just a few of the stories of the kids at Hope. To see these kids in person would never reveal what they had been through. They laugh, play, joke, tease, run, and jump just like most normal children. Hearing about what happened to them made me feel awful, and I felt sorry for them. However, they aren't feeling sorry for themselves.

These kids are an inspiration to us all. They were victims of circumstance, out of their control, but they aren't allowing that time period to define who they are. They recognize today's blessings from God and embrace them with gratefulness. They are not allowing what God has blessed them with today to be tainted by what satan has attempted to destroy yesterday.

There were two kids that tugged on my heart during my stay at Hope – Humza and Juliet. Humza was an annoying little kid who weighed about as much as a small sack of potatoes and was somehow always filthy. He was very territorial, and I had to get on to him a couple of times for not letting other kids hold my hand. Somehow, even through his rough exterior, Humza found a way into my heart. Like all of the kids, he just wanted attention and love.

The other kid was Juliet, whom I talked about earlier. She was about 12 years old and had a sweet smile and loving heart. I wrote a little about her in my blog:

> "This was the last day at Hope Children's Home. It hit me harder than I expected it to. One of the girls that I got to know well came and gave me a hug goodbye, and she had tears in her eyes. She tried to hide that she was wiping them away. She would not leave my side until we left. I would adopt her if I could. I'm terribly sad just thinking about it.
>
> Before I left, the pastor came up to me and told me that she thought I should get a visa and stay here. I laughed and showed her pictures of my family that I'm coming home to and that I miss greatly. Before I got in the van to leave, she again came up to me and told me that I should stay here.
>
> A big piece of me did. I will never be the same."

Pastor Prossy was in charge of Hope, and she was also in charge of the church on the grounds. She was with us when we went to the prison to minister, and we got to know her well. She loves these kids so much.

I was really touched when we were about to leave. She came up to me saying that I should stay. She said that everybody else could go home, but that I needed to stay. I almost hate to type it out for fear that someone from my team would get their feelings hurt, but she said it that powerfully to me. I was taken back by it. The fact that she said it again was equally as shocking to me. Although I didn't know it yet, God would use those words by Pastor Prossy to shape my future.

(Two girls at Hope Children's Home)
Photo taken by Julie LaPat

Chapter 12

Juliet & Humza

When we arrived back from Uganda, we had a fanfare of a welcome in the airport. My kids had made me a banner, and it felt so great to be back on American soil. I was relieved to see my wife and kids, extended family, and familiar faces again. Finally! Our mission was complete, and we were all home safe. I couldn't wait to get home and take a hot shower. I was totally exhausted.

If you have ever worn glasses or contacts, you know that when you wake up in the morning, one of the first things you do is put them on. They allow you to see everything clearer. That was what it was like after returning home. I was wearing a new pair of glasses and seeing things from a new perspective. At first I thought that it was just jet lag, but as time passed by, I slowly realized that God had changed me.

I was told that that feeling will go away after about 6 months and that I will return to normal. That was kind of a sad and scary statement to me at the time.

After what I witnessed, how could I ever be the same? As time went on, however, I became more and more depressed. I can't really explain why depression was the overwhelming emotion to me at that time, but it was. My kids recently told me that I wasn't the same when I returned from Uganda. I slept more and didn't laugh as much. I didn't tease them very much either (which is not like me at all). There was a burden on my heart, and this burden eventually started a "wrestling period" with God that hasn't ended to this day.

Remember Juliet and Humza? About a week after I returned from Africa, Amy and I prayerfully decided to pursue adopting them. I wrote an email to the organization asking them the same. The following is part of the email:

> "We just ask that you prayerfully consider this request. We know that, if allowed, there are many hoops to jump through and that it will be expensive. We are willing to do whatever it takes if it's the Lord's will."

They agreed to prayerfully consider our request. We were excited that they didn't refuse our request right away, but then came the hard part – waiting. Waiting is one of the most difficult things to do in stressful situations. A couple of weeks later we got a response that the board had decided to pray again for a week to try to get God's heart for this issue. Then we heard what began to become a familiar phrase in Uganda's orphanages: "Our heart has always been to help raise up the kids… to be leaders in Uganda."

That phrase really struck a cord with me. It sounds so good and so right. Kind of right along the lines of "feed a man a fish and feed him for a day, but teach a man to fish and feed him for a lifetime." There are many organizations in Uganda that have the same mindset - to train the kids to be Christian leaders in their community.

While it sounds great and all, I disagree with it if it prevents those children from having a Christian forever family. Part of my reply to his email was:

> "What is best for the child – to become a leader for the community, or to have a consistent and stable family for the rest of their lives?"

Are we the ones to decide who becomes a leader? No. God chooses who becomes a leader. God chose Abraham, God chose Jacob, God chose Joseph, God chose Moses, and God chose David. All of these men were given circumstances that would make them an unlikely candidate to becoming a great leader. Abraham was childless, Jacob was a deceiver, Joseph was a slave, Moses had a speech impediment, and David was the least of the shepherd boys. However, God still chose them to become leaders.

How about training these children to be great Christian moms and dads, husbands and wives? How about putting them in Christian homes to learn to become great *servants* and *followers* of Jesus? Think about it this way. What if those were your children in the orphanage? Would your top concern for them be that they become community leaders?

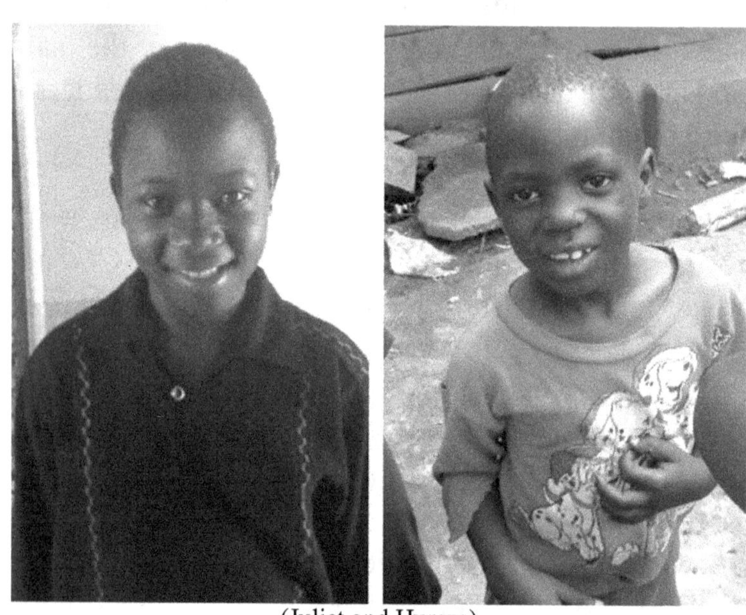
(Juliet and Humza)
Photo taken by Amy Collins

During the waiting period, we even offered to become the pioneers to formulate the adoption process and become the adoption agency for this organization. We were ready to do whatever it took.

A few weeks later we got the news. The organization, as nicely as they could, stated that they "did not feel a peace in the decision of allowing adoptions…"

We were devastated. We couldn't wrap our minds around the reality that Juliet and Humza would never have a forever family. It is very hard to think about even to this day. Knowing that their answer was final, I solemnly replied:

> "While saying that we are disappointed would be grossly understated, I do want to thank you for your time and prayerful consideration. Please convey our gratitude to the rest of the… team and board as we understand that many hours of prayer, discussion, and research went into this decision."

My wife ended up getting to meet Juliet and Humza about a year later. This is what she wrote after seeing them:

> "Have you ever searched for God, sought His heart? Then, feeling His tug inside, prayed for something, even begged and pleaded with tears, only to find that the answer is 'not now' or maybe even 'no'?
>
> Have you ever wondered about God's reasoning in all this? Why the change in direction? Why the ebb and flow? Why the mystery of His ways?
>
> Have you ever had a stretch of time pass after these happenings, and then revisited them, only

to see that time has marched on, and the changes are apparent.

I am so glad that I am not God! I am so glad that HE has the whole world in His hands! Every person, every child, every orphan. So, in these moments, I try to rest in the fact that there is a time for everything. And the tears flow, and heaven seems like such a perfect place."

"There is a time for everything, and a season for every activity under the heavens:

a time to be born and a time to die,
a time to plant and a time to uproot,
a time to kill and a time to heal,
a time to tear down and a time to build,
a time to weep and a time to laugh,
a time to mourn and a time to dance,
a time to scatter stones and
a time to gather them,
a time to embrace and
a time to refrain from embracing,
a time to search and a time to give up,
a time to keep and a time to throw away,
a time to tear and a time to mend,
a time to be silent and a time to speak,
a time to love and a time to hate,
a time for war and a time for peace.

He has made everything beautiful in its time. He has also set eternity in the hearts of men; yet they cannot fathom what God has done from beginning to end." Ecclesiastes 3:1-8, 11

Chapter 13

It's Not all Roses

"And we know that in all things God works for the good of those who love him, who have been called according to his purpose." Romans 8:28

After I had returned from Africa and we were told we could not adopt the two children that we fell in love with at the orphanage, I was depressed for about a month. It was a depression that was filled with struggle and anxiety, almost like I was wrestling with God about something that I didn't understand. After much prayer and discussion, Amy and I decided that we were called as a family to become missionaries to Uganda to help children get adopted into forever families. We finally had direction and a hope for the future! There was this giant surge of relief and peace that could only be expressed in joy and excitement.

What we didn't realize was that not everyone felt the joy and excitement that we felt. When I think back about it, how could they? Everyone did not experience Uganda and the miracles I saw. Everyone did not go through the struggle that we just went through. Everyone was not told that the children they loved were unadoptable. Everyone did not just have a giant burden lifted off of their shoulders and experience the peace that comes with knowing part of the plan that God had revealed.

When Amy and I told each of our families that we were called to be missionaries, as is imaginable, there were a lot of tough questions and varied reactions. Then there was the silence as if we had not mentioned going at all. These were the dark times. I'm not sure what we were expecting, but we were feeling more discouraged with each passing day. It was during these times that I learned how satan uses miscommunication to attack strong Christian families.

Looking back, we are able to see how our families did not want us to get hurt and wanted to be sure of what God was doing in our lives. In essence, they wanted to be a part of what God was doing. They wanted to feel our calling themselves in a way that would allow them to get excited in the Spirit. But we did not understand this. In turn, feelings got hurt and more feelings got hurt. Things began to spiral downward with seemingly nobody in the cockpit. Believe me when I say that our hands did not stay clean in all of this. We made mistakes, and there are things we wish we could do over. Mistakes were made on all sides, and the family divisions were growing larger.

There was one verse that kept coming to mind during all of this, and it was Ephesians 6:12:

> "For our struggle is not against flesh and blood, but against the rulers, against the authorities, against the powers of this dark world and against the spiritual forces of evil in the heavenly realms."

What was clear on many fronts was that there was a spiritual battle we were neither prepared for nor had the knowledge to fight. This was something only God could conquer. It was beyond our comprehension, beyond our scope of thought, beyond words, it was something that only the King of Kings and Lord of Lords could battle.

Thankfully, God did battle for us – and by us I mean for all of our family. He did not allow satan to destroy our relationships, but instead used those hardships to guide us and direct us toward where He wanted us to be.

I wish I could say that everything is perfect now, but it's not. There were apologies made and forgiveness granted, but we are human, and some things take time. Situations have greatly improved, and we all have hope that they will continue to do so. We are blessed to have extended family that is committed to Jesus. Because of that, we each do our best to forgive, forget, and give others the grace and mercy that He afforded to us.

Chapter 14

Beautiful Feet

About a year had passed since I had returned from that life changing mission trip to Uganda, and about nine months since we answered the call to go there as missionaries. The call to go to Uganda wasn't just a blanket calling. It was pretty specific. One day we wrote it out, and this is what it said:

> "We strive to share the love of Christ by promoting Christian families for orphans, assisting in caring for orphans, helping orphanages provide the best possible care and communication, and offering encouragement to adoptive families that will enable children to be taught and shown the Gospel of God's love for a lifetime. In doing this, we hope to further Christ's kingdom in the lives of orphans, to provide support to Christian adoptive couples on their complex journey, to assist over burdened orphanages, and to witness and minister to the local community through preaching, teaching, worship, and discipleship."

In short, God wanted us to be used to help promote, encourage, and support Ugandan orphan adoptions into Christian families. Over the past 9 months since answering God's call to become missionaries, we were finding out that it was very difficult to be matched to an organization with the same mission and mindset that needed help. We searched and searched but kept coming up empty handed. We contacted about 45 different Christian Ugandan organizations!

It is tempting to drudge on and on about the hardships that aspiring missionaries have and the hurdles that they must jump over just to do what God has called them to do. However, that is saying, to some degree, that the door God opens is better than the door God closes. This, simply, is just not true. God shut so many doors that when He finally opened one, we were confident about stepping through it.

There were two or three "doors" that we thought might possibly be open by this point in our journey. My sister, Julie, who led the mission trip to Uganda earlier, was going there to adopt a little girl. My wife, Amy, was going with her for a couple reasons. First, she was going to help Julie and get to know the Ugandan adoption process. Secondly, she was going to scope out a few organizations that we thought might be possibilities. This is what she wrote about her initial experience:

> "I have always wanted to go to Africa. Yet, knowing that I was leaving my family for 25 days left me crying myself to sleep on Wednesday night. I keep telling God that I am not adequate to do the things that He asks of me. And He keeps telling me that 'I can do everything through (Christ) who gives me strength' (Philippians 4:13) and '(His) power is made perfect in weakness' (2 Corinthians 12:9) and 'The God who made the world and everything in it is the Lord of heaven and earth and does not live in temples built by man. He is not served by humans hands as if He needed anything because He Himself gives men life and breath and everything else' (Acts 17:24, 25) So really the journey of following Him to the places He has for me, these 25 days it is Uganda, is not about ME and what I can do, but about HIM and taking a seat in the front row to see all that brings Him glory."

It is interesting to point out that Amy says that she has "always wanted to go to Africa." When she was in elementary, she went to a church camp, and the pastor asked the kids to come forward if they wanted to commit their lives to ministry. My wife answered that alter call and went forward. She prayed with a young pastor and felt God was calling her to be a missionary to Africa some day. Here she was, about 30 years later, and God was providing that opportunity.

(Amy holding Frank while swinging)
Photo taken by Julie LaPat

Amy stayed in the guest house of the orphanage where Julie's daughter lived. It's amazing to hear of the needs of these children. Amy writes:

"I didn't have a lot of dreamt up ideas about what orphanage life is like. So, meeting about 50 children under the age of 5 who are orphans was heart wrenching to take in. The moment I walked in the room, one little guy with slightly crossed eyes put his hands up for me to hold him. It was instant love!! That has happened now with ALL the children. They are so precious! They do fight over attention and want to be the ONLY one a mile around being held. During much of their weekend time and their play times during the week, they play outside in the beautiful Ugandan weather. The mobile ones get where they want to go on the terraced yard with a sand pit and slide. The others play on a mat under a gazebo with a tiled floor. Even the newborns are napping on a blanket on the ground…

So, what's so heart wrenching? Well, these children need so much love. The staff does the best they can, but the "mommas" (the women who take care of the orphans) work 12 hour shifts, often 7 days a week, getting paid about $45 a month... Needless to say, the kids are clamoring for hugs and kisses.

One little boy was given a picture book of his

adoptive family. He didn't put it down all day. He showed it to everyone he saw, squealing if any other kid got close to it. This is his only possession. He does not have his own clothes, toys, or blanket. But, he was old enough to know he had a family who will be coming to get him and take him home…

(These little kids) are the least of these with nothing of their own. Even their name is often unknown and temporary. But, I pray it is only a matter of a short time until their forever mommies and daddies come to take them to their forever homes!

As I spend more time with the orphans, I am realizing that giving love means giving my heart, of course. So, the more I choose to give, the harder it will be to walk away. Is it worth it?

I read last night in Acts 20:19 'I served the Lord with great humility and with tears…', which was written about Paul. So, I was reassured to confirm that the tears of serving Jesus are normal, probably even standard protocol.

My dear friend sent me the verse from Isaiah 52:7 'How beautiful on the mountains are the feet of those who bring good news, who proclaim peace, who bring good tidings, who proclaim salvation, who say to Zion, 'Your God reigns!'

> When reading this verse and reflecting on the scenes of severe poverty as we would see it in America and even thinking about my very dirty feet, I am so thankful that God doesn't see beauty the same way I do. The children at Hope are beautiful, not because of the clothes they wear or the bows in their hair but because they are loved by God. He doesn't see them as beautiful someday when..... He sees them as beautiful now."

It's amazing to think that a great and mighty God, so powerful and awe inspiring, looks at these children and sees them as "beautiful now." Many of these kids have HIV and other diseases and physical or mental problems, and God still sees them as beautiful. If He sees them as beautiful, don't you think He sees you as beautiful too?

Chapter 15

The Search

Now it was time for Amy to get to work while she was in Uganda. She had a limited amount of time to find and analyze these organizations. Some were hours away from where she was staying, and she was determined to find them. This is what she writes:

> "When reading a book, I am one of those people who can hardly skim a word, let alone skip to the last chapter to read the end without reading the chapters in between. However, when it comes to the story of my life, I have been very tempted to want to skip pages to see what is next. I don't think I would hesitate to even read the end if I could! This must be why God doesn't allow me to know the future ahead of time. By waiting on Him to reveal the next chapter, even the next word, He is able to write the story of my life without me making editorial changes, which is a very good thing! I know I would make a mess of it for sure!
>
> Today, Julie and I spent over 12 hours searching

for the next chapter. Charlie and I and the kids have been praying hard about how and where God wants us to serve in Uganda. This is a meticulous and faith building process to say the least. However, I am thankful that God allowed us to find two organizations today that are wonderfully run and like-minded in being pro-adoption of older children. Both of these places were elusive of ease or smooth roads and took many boda-boda drivers and other random people to help us find them. Yet, God is good all the time! He was faithful to help us, and I am renewed with excitement to see what He is up to in the next chapter!"

"… And let us run with perseverance the race marked out for us, fixing our eyes on Jesus, the pioneer and perfecter of faith. For the joy set before Him He endured the cross, scorning its shame, and sat down at the right hand of the throne of God. Consider Him who endured such opposition from sinners, so that you will not grow weary and lose heart." Hebrews 12:1b-3

Amy had done it! We had hope that at least one of these organizations would be a match. Was this where God was calling us, or did He have something else in mind? Only time would tell. However, Amy's trip with my sister wasn't over and something unexpected happened. Amy goes on to write:

“A huge aspect of the trip that I didn’t foresee was falling in love with a certain little orphan named Maria. I really should have known this would be a job hazard of serving at an orphanage. Less than a year before my trip, Charlie had come home feeling burdened for two kids needing a family. Of course, I would feel the same tug at my heart. Maria was about two years old and had bright eyes and a determined scowl. She had scrawny legs, a poochy belly, and scrubby hair (they shave all the children’s hair short at the orphanage). Even though she couldn’t walk, she would scoot her way to the playground to join the other toddlers. Relishing in the love she so craved and needed, she would hold me tight and giggle a smoker’s laugh. No other child was welcome to share my lap. Maria wanted my attention all to herself.

On coming home, I told Charlie of little Maria, who stole my heart. He approved of seeking from the Lord and also the orphanage director whether or not she could be added to our family. We started the adoption process with anticipation. I started to fervently pray that God would give her a loving, Christian family. In less than a month, we were told that she had been matched to another American family. This is what I wrote in my prayer journal:

‘You know I wholeheartedly love Maria. And, although the director of the orphanage (makes

> the decisions), You have all authority, and You place children (the lonely) in families, and You know what is best. I can trust You. I can trust You. You know my heart more than even I do. You know what is best. You are good all the time. I grieve Maria. I love her. And You love her more. You know best.'

The feeling of not adopting Maria was very reminiscent of when we could not adopt Juliet and Humza about one year earlier, especially for Amy. We had started the home study and adoption process only to find out a month later that she was not available. While we had joy knowing Maria would now have a Christian family, it was still a difficult time for us. With a broken heart, we continued to search for where God was leading.

Chapter 15

The River

If there was ever a time in our lives that we needed to pull back on the throttle of life, this was it. We were juggling 10 balls at once, and there were 10 more on the table waiting for their turn. We were trying to sell our house, holding garage sales, buying supplies, getting passports, looking for sending agencies, and a mountain of other things you can think of trying to get ready to move to Uganda as a family of six.

We would clean our house for a showing, and then it would get all messed up 10 minutes later. We would clean it again for another showing, and the same thing would happen again. This was an endless cycle. It always seemed like there was somebody waiting for our kids to dump out all of their toy boxes and for the laundry to be piled high, and then they would want to see the house within the next 30 minutes. It was driving us crazy!

Our solution, and God's provision, was to move to "The River." The River is a house that my parents own situated along the South Canadian River. It is 20 minutes from any city or town and there is

(Isaac driving “Ole Blue”)

(Peaceful view of The River)

farmland all around. It is breathtakingly beautiful, especially during the changing of the seasons. After opening the gate to enter the property, there is a winding decent through a thick cover of trees until arriving at the house. Once at the house, the trees open up and you can see far out into the valley. About 300 yards away, you can see the South Canadian River.

We hadn't realized it yet, but the River was a sanctuary for us during this difficult time. It was quiet and beautiful. It forced us to take a step back. We decided to break off some of our responsibilities at church, home school co-ops, sports, and other activities. Being there allowed us to slow down and give ourselves a chance to think and to pray. I can't think of a better place to be when needing to hear God speak.

God blessed us during this time. We lived the country life and enjoyed every minute of it. Our kids got chickens, and there was daily excitement when one would lay an egg. We would load up in my old 1986 GMC pickup we call "Ole Blue" and go feed the cows with my dad, or "Papa" as the kids call him. He had planted a few rows of grapes and they apparently drank a lot of water because my dad would always need to "check on the grapes" – which we knew meant that we were all going to go water them for the next 45 minutes. Our kids still joke about "checking on the grapes." Of course, they didn't mind it much because Papa would buy them a huge coke at the Indian Trading Post when they were done.

On cold nights, I would start a fire in the fireplace, and it would heat up the entire living room. We would all take turns standing by the fireplace to warm up, and we loved watching the warm glow of the flames kiss the glass on the door.

A few weeks before Christmas, we hiked out into the valley just before the river looking for a Christmas tree. It didn't take long before we found it, and the kids started to cut it down. We loaded it on the four-wheeler and hauled it back to the house. The kids decorated it with lights and even made ornaments out of spent red shotgun shells. There's no such thing as a perfect Christmas tree and, if you are going by looks, there's no such thing as anywhere near a perfect Christmas tree at the River. However, we had so much fun, and it looked so pathetically cute. It was about the most perfect Christmas tree I can ever remember.

The River doesn't make for an amazing and awe inspiring story to tell. But it does deserve a chapter in this book because it was an important chapter in our lives. God used the River as a blessing to us when we needed it the most. We needed the solace and peace that the River offered like no other time in our lives. It allowed us to think clearer, listen harder, and grow closer like no other place ever could have.

Chapter 16

Unanswered Questions

Approaching a year after answering God's call to be missionaries, we were still struggling with finding where and how God wanted us to go. We were in the middle of a stressful situation, and the doors all around us were closed. Our house wouldn't sell, we couldn't find an organization that fit what we were called to do, we hadn't even thought about fundraising yet, and sadly enough, I started to feel shame when people would ask about it. This was what I wrote on June 24th, 2012 in my blog:

> "It has been about four months since Amy returned from Uganda to help my sister adopt Lucy and to visit orphanages. She visited these orphanages to see if there were some that would need our help and that would be a good fit for our family. There was one that she wanted to make sure she got to see. It was in a town called Jinja, and it was very hard to find. She about gave up, but she finally found it. She thought it was amazing and loved the children and the

atmosphere. They are adoption minded, and they even place older children. These were two things we were looking for because that is what we were called to help with in Uganda. A few days later, she visited them again and spent the night. Her feelings for them were even more confirmed. Upon hearing about this orphanage, I was super excited because we had spent so many months looking for a place to serve that was in line with what God called us to do.

When Amy returned home, we were excited to pursue this opportunity. We were told we would receive an application to fill out. We waited. After a while, we skyped the director. She said she was excited about us and that she would talk to the board and send us an application. We waited. After a while, we sent emails and phoned and then waited some more. About a month and a half ago, we finally talked to a couple people on the ground in the U.S. affiliated with the orphanage, and the conversation went well. They said that they would send an application, and they did. We sent it in... and waited. About a week ago, we agreed that if we didn't hear anything from them by this Sunday, June 24th, that we would not work with this orphanage. Here it is, Sunday June 24th as I type this, and I am hoping and praying we will hear something... get some kind of email... or some kind of phone call.

After church today, we did what we try to do as a family on Sundays - Family Forum. It's a time where we can all bring up something we want to talk about without fear of getting into trouble. Most of the time it's about getting something, buying something, or doing something. Today was no different, but then we started talking about Uganda and that we may have eliminated the only real option that is on the table. I asked them what they thought about it. This was when it got difficult. Brandy said that maybe God doesn't want us to go. Brandon said that maybe we should give them more time. Cody thought the same. I told them that if we are supposed to go through them that God will allow us to hear something but that we have to be open to what God has in store for us. Maybe that it's not to go or to wait.

Then Cody said, 'It just seems like a waste.' I said, 'What is a waste?' He said, 'That we did all of that work, and packed all of our toys, and gave away a bunch of our toys to just not go. We have come this far. I think we should go.' Cody started to cry. I did too. Brandon brought up that God promised Abraham a son, and it took a long time for Abraham to get his son. Cody said, 'Yeah, and Paul didn't give up when he was a missionary.' Brandy also said that she thought we should still go. Brandon then quoted Jeremiah 29:11 'For I know the plans I have for you,' declares the Lord, 'plans to prosper you and not to harm you, plans to give you hope and a future.'

And then Isaac said something about Disneyland and the Toy Story ride, and we all laughed.

We left it that we are going to pray and fast one day this week about God's role in our lives in Uganda. There are so many unanswered questions - and we desperately need guidance. Please pray with us."

Chapter 17

What's Next?

A few months later, it was becoming more and more clear to us that our options to serve as missionaries in Uganda, while fulfilling the calling that God gave us, were dwindling. On September 21, 2012, I write:

> "First and foremost, we praise God and give Him the glory for all the things He has shown us and done through us. He is always faithful, always loving, and He continues to show us that.
>
> For about the last year and a half, our family has been trying to fulfill God's calling on our lives to go to Uganda and share Christ's love to orphans and adoptive families. While we never imagined the obstacles that would come our way or how incredibly difficult the journey would prove to be, we have come to the conclusion that we have been blessed throughout the entire time. As my wife has continued to remind me, 'It's not about us.' God has shown us His grace and mercy at times when we were about to

break or about to give up. He would give us strength and let us know that He was in control even though we did not understand what was going on. Who are we that our Creator should care enough to want to bring us comfort during times of stress? Who are we that the Lord of Lords should stoop so low to bring us peace? I don't know the answer to those questions, but it raises another: Who could deny the mercy that God extends when He loves and cares for us so much?

At the beginning of August, Amy and I prayerfully came up with a much needed plan for our next steps. This is what we wrote:

'We will wait for the house listing to fully run through. If the house sells, we plan to do our best to find a place to serve, fundraise, and go. If it doesn't sell, but we have found a place to serve, we will do what measures it takes to go regardless of the house. If the house doesn't sell, and there are no clear leads, then we plan to move back in the house and serve God from here.'

A couple weeks before the end of our house listing, an orphanage organization based out of Tulsa called us. We sent them an application, and they wanted to meet us. About the same time, we were planning on moving back home and complete the granite countertop installation among other home projects. The countertops that came in were not what we ordered, and I was very upset about it. Why did it feel like everything was breaking and every small task so big?

A day or two after our house went off the market and we took the sign down, a guy called wanting to look at it. I told him that the kitchen was a complete mess because the countertops were ripped out. He said his wife would want to choose the countertops and backsplash anyway. Amy and I didn't know what to think. We gave it to God and left it up to Him. We were willing to stay or go, and we were excited to know what His plan was for us.

We met with the organization's board on September 9th and got to know each of them and their passion for ministry in Uganda. They called us later and wanted us to give them a proposal of what we wanted to do in Uganda. We sent three 'ideas' to them, and they will be discussing them in the coming weeks and get back to us.

Meanwhile, the guy that wanted to buy the house has since stopped communicating. He made a low offer, and we countered and that was the end of that - so it seems.

Once again we are back to the unknown and the waiting. Waiting is hard to do, especially for extended periods of time. Waiting is hard to do when it doesn't seem logical. Why wait when we could be doing something or making progress? Believe me, we've gone through the range of emotions, the sin of impatience, the selfish thoughts, and the complaining. But in the end, God knows, and His timing is perfect. If it were up to me, I probably wouldn't have made the Jews wander around in the desert for 40 years. That doesn't seem logical, but it was perfect for what God wanted it to accomplish. In the end, Moses didn't get to even enter the Promised Land. We are prepared for the same fate. Does that mean Moses wasted his time? It might have felt like it to Him but in God's grand plan, it wasn't.

As we struggle with where to go from here, we remember our plan we made in August and tread toward that side of the lake. We plan to move back home. This could take a while because of all of the repairs to do, but it will also give us time to evaluate the organization we talked with. There are a few things that are important for us to tell whomever may be interested:

1) We accepted 3 checks during this time from people wanting to support us. We greatly appreciate this support (and we really mean

that). However, we did not cash any of them because we did not want to accept money without a firm plan in place.

2) We said we were going to go to Uganda to be missionaries. If we don't, we lied. This is unacceptable. Our kids have worked so hard for this, and it is not right to tell people one thing and do another. If all doors close on us going to Uganda as long-term missionaries, we plan to still take a short-term mission trip to Uganda as a family.

3) God is good. This may be a test of faith for us, something to make us stronger for the future, a way for us to gain insight that we needed, or to open a door down the road that we don't even know about. We don't deny our calling. We wouldn't have moved and gone through this if we weren't 100% sure that God called us to do it. Just because we don't know where He is taking us, doesn't mean we don't know who is driving. We praise Him and give Him the glory!"

The very next day, I get a call from the guy interested in our house. This is what I write about it:

"…I got a call from the guy that was interested in our house. We had talked a week earlier, and he made a low offer. Amy and I countered it, and he said he would call us back to let us know. He didn't call us back until a week later. By that point, we thought it was over. We were wrong. He said he would take the house at the price I offered him. Big Jesus! With our house being off the market for almost a month after 14 months of trying to sell it, without a sign in the yard, without realtors, and with a house with a broken water heater, and without kitchen countertops and the backsplash all torn out, with a dishwasher needing repair, with a microwave needing repair, and with a water well needing repair, we got a contract on our house! We sold it AS-IS for more than what we thought we'd get. God is amazing!

> Not having a realtor saved us 6% in fees. The price we got was almost exactly 6% less than what we originally listed our house for 15 months ago - a difference of $170."

At this time, we didn't know why God was selling our house, but He was! We had no clue what was around the corner. Here is what I write about it on November 12, 2012:

> "It's hard to believe, but we are supposed to close on our house tomorrow! 7 weeks and 4 closing dates later, it might really happen. The difficult part is where to go from here. The organization that showed an interest in us in August let us know a few weeks ago that they decided that they weren't ready for a missionary

family. That possibility was one of the reasons why we decided to sell our house. Combine that with the miraculous way our house sold, and we know that it was supposed to happen. But the question remains... why? Why did God want us to sell our house? Was it so that we would just buy another one? We aren't sure, but we do know that there is something exciting around the corner. REALLY exciting. We are hopeful that it will be the fulfillment of what God has called us to do in Uganda.

We will do what it takes. We WILL keep going. Philippians 4:13 'I can do everything through him who gives me strength.'

God is faithful. He is true. Throughout all of the turmoil and stress in the past 2 years, He has guided us and comforted us and protected us. Satan has used the tools at his disposal to try to chip away at our faith and destroy us as Christians. I laugh in his face because he has already been defeated through the resurrection of Jesus. Faith in Christ is true strength and real power. We praise Him and give Him the glory for this time in our lives."

Chapter 18

An Open Door

God is always and continually faithful even when we can't see what is ahead, and He alone deserves all of the praise and glory. On January 4th, 2013, I write:

> "God has closed so many doors throughout the past year and a half that we thought we were not going to go to Uganda - at least we thought for now. We had decided to move back into our house at the end of August and then God miraculously sold our house. We were confused as to why He did that since we had no plans to go to Uganda. It makes more sense now. If we had moved back into our house, we would've been closed to what He had in mind for us. He wasn't done with us yet.
>
> Amy's friend was in Uganda a couple months ago adopting a child, and Amy asked her if there were other children that she knew of that needed a family. She said there were two sisters needing to be adopted, ages 5 and 3. We prayed about it and got in touch with the adoption

agency. They were very helpful, and we started the process. We applied to the adoption agency, and we were accepted. We re-started our homestudy and are currently in the process of gathering all of the required information for international adoption. We plan on going to Uganda this spring with our kids to bring their sisters home. God has provided all along. His plans are perfect. God WAS opening doors for us and because of so many closed doors, it was confirmation that we were doing what He wanted. As if to give us even more encouragement, we found out that someone donated to the agency to help with our adoption expenses. This was shocking to us since we hadn't told very many people that we were adopting and even fewer people the name of the agency we are using.

As you can imagine, taking Amy and I and 4 kids to Uganda and bringing 6 kids back is expensive. Combine this with the adoption fees, and it easily becomes very overwhelming. God has provided once again in a very big way. Yesterday, I was handed a check for almost the exact amount it will take to cover our costs! Cody said, "That's an answered prayer!" Brandy said, "Now we *know* God wants us to adopt them!" As the saying goes, "God is rarely early, but He is never late." We are soooo glad that He is in control!!!!"

Chapter 19

God Provides

We were going to leave for Uganda in about a month to bring our new daughters and sisters home. Wait a minute! We didn't have a home to bring them to! We were still living at the River, and we knew that we needed a house. God already had that problem solved, and we didn't even realize it.

You see, we had put a contract on a house in Mustang, Oklahoma. It was on 5 acres, and included a swimming pool, a pond, a shop, and all of the extras. We all thought it was great! It *was* great until the AC units got stolen, the hot water tank broke, and we found out that the roof was bad – not to mention that it was already more than we wanted to pay.

Even after all that was going wrong with this house, I still had my mind set on it. It wasn't until one day that we were sitting in my mom and dad's living room, talking to the kids, that we figured out what to do.

About a month earlier, my mom and dad had quickly put a contract on the house next door to theirs since houses in the area normally sell really fast. They did this because they knew of a relative that wanted to live in this area, and so they wanted to snatch it up before someone else purchased it. It turned out that this relative opted not to buy the house.

So while we were sitting in my parents' living room, talking to our kids, I asked them, "Would you rather live on 5 acres, have a pool, a shop, and a pond or live next door to Mimi and Papa?" Unanimously they exclaimed, "Live next to Mimi and Papa!" We thought, "What in the world are we doing?" and we closed on the house next door two weeks later.

God provided again! He literally sold our old house for us and bought our new house for us as well!!! He is absolutely amazing and provides for His children if only they will look to Him!

Now, our "new" house needed a ton of work. It only had 3 bedrooms, and the kitchen was really small. The guest bathroom was purple, and unless I could convince my kids that Barney was still cool, we were going to have to gut it.

A week later, Amy's dad and aunt came down from South Dakota and Nebraska to help with the house. With the help from a young couple at church and family, we added a room, expanded the kitchen, remodeled the guest bathroom, and painted the interior of the house in a matter of three weeks! The flooring and appliances would be installed while we were in Uganda. Although there was more to do when we returned from Uganda in order to move in, God provided. He provided a home for our family.

I never thought I would live in this house – a house that I passed thousands of times as a kid living right next door. However, God used this house to show us His faithfulness and to also give us hope and healing. Right at the time when we needed it the most, God opened the floodgates and family and friends came out of the woodwork and showered us with love and support.

Chapter 20

Missionaries at Last

It was March 14th, 2013, and we were boarding a plane that would begin our journey to Uganda as a family! Wow! This was it! I can't explain to you the excitement that we felt as we all took our seats. Our kids were entertaining to watch as they marveled at their first flight, peaking out of the plane's windows. Their amazement, however, started to dwindle with each following leg of the journey.

We had a 24-hour layover in Belgium, which is where one of our flooring suppliers for our family business makes its product. My dad lined up a tour of the factory in advance, and so they came and picked us up at the airport. We received the most amazing tour of Belgium and even toured the old square area at night and ate at a genuine Belgian restaurant complete with a menu choice of "calf brain." The kids got a big kick out of that.

We had a brief stop in Rwanda, and then to Uganda. As our jet touched down in Uganda, I thought to myself, "Whatever happens here, we have fulfilled

(Brandy, Brandon, Cody, and Isaac about to leave for Uganda)

(All of us in front of the Town Hall in Brussels, Belgium)

our calling." It is hard to imagine, but just by getting to Uganda as a family, a huge weight and relief was lifted from my shoulders.

This relief was short-lived to some degree because we found out that all of our luggage had been lost. All we had were our backpacks that we carried on the plane. Thankfully, we had a backup plan inside the backpacks in case our luggage got lost, but it would still be difficult.

After landing in the middle of the night, we were riding from the airport to the guest house with a driver that we had never met. Nightlife in Uganda in the city is not quiet and peaceful. There are many people walking around, fires in trash cans, street vendors, hair salons buzzing, and bars open with many people hanging around. As we were driving down the road, there was a man lying in the ditch who appeared to be dead. People were just walking and driving by like he didn't exist, and we were about to do the same. This is what I later wrote:

> "Also, please pray for the guy laying on the side of the road. I asked our driver what happened to him, and he thought he saw a car ahead of us swerve, so he probably got hit. I told him that we needed to turn around and help him. He laughed and said that then everyone would say he did it and that the police would drive by eventually. I asked him if he might die. He laughed and said yes. I said that it was terrible

> and didn't talk to him the rest of the time. A few miles after that a boda boda (motorcycle) going at least 45-50 mpg hit a dog and almost crashed. The dog limped off."

I found out recently that my daughter, Brandy, was really mad at me at that point because I didn't force him to turn around. I can definitely understand her anger because I was angry with the driver as well. However, I was in no position at that time to press the situation. We were in a third world country. My entire family was in the vehicle. It was at night, and I didn't know the driver… need I say more?

We finally crashed at the boarding house and slept for what felt like 15 minutes, then we were off to Fort Portal to finally get to meet Sarah and Faith!

Chapter 21

Sarah & Faith

Here we were, the day that we were going to meet our two new daughters. We were very excited and felt somewhat rested after a good night's sleep. We were staying at a place called "Ataco," and the rooms were actually little modernized huts complete with thatched roofs. Each hut had two apartments, and there was a porch with chairs to enjoy the view. In front of the huts, there was a beautiful courtyard where the kids would play soccer and run around. This is what Amy says about the long awaited meeting of our daughters:

> "After eating a nice, big breakfast at Ataco, the place that we stayed the night in Fort Portal, the six of us loaded in the driver's mini van to go to Ibonde Children's Home. Anticipating the long awaited meeting with our two new daughters, the drive seemed to go on forever. We pulled up to the orphanage about 30 minutes later. We waited in a small office with a few chairs, a computer, and a printer in order to meet the orphanage director. After exchanging

(Sarah and Faith in their bright yellow uniforms at school)

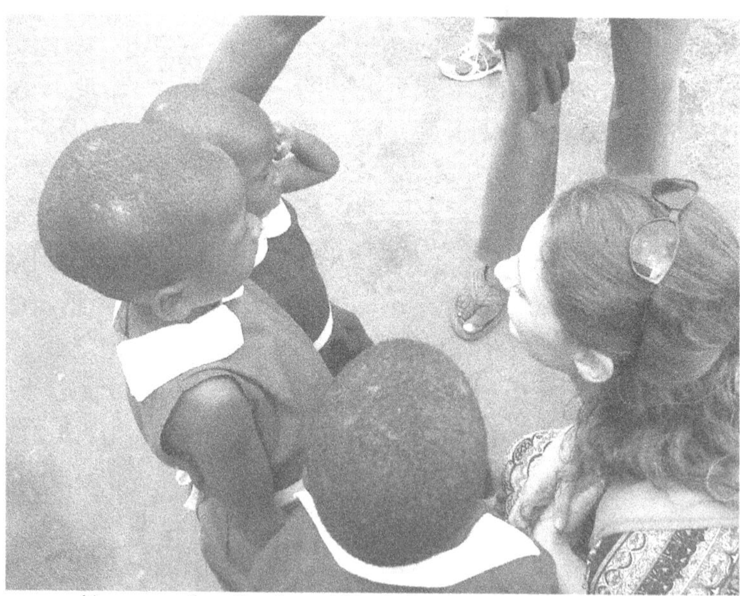

(Amy meeting Sarah and Faith for the very first time)

formalities with the orphanage directors and signing the guest book, it was finally time to meet the girls. They were at the partnering school across the street. We crossed the road, walked past a modest office area, and entered a bustling schoolyard full of young students wearing blue and yellow uniforms. Immediately, we started scanning the many happy, active faces to find the ones that matched the few pictures we had stared at for months. Brandy suddenly exclaimed, "There they are! There's Sarah and Faith!" Sure enough, they were a few feet from us, approaching slowly and smiling sheepishly. I don't even remember what I first said or did. Other kids started to gather around. They were especially amused by our kids. Isaac was bombarded with kids touching his red hair and pinching his white skin. We went to see Sarah's classroom and meet her teacher. Soon, we were standing at the gate to the school, taking a picture as a family of 8, with two Ugandan girls in blue and yellow uniforms in our arms.

We left the schoolyard to go back to the orphanage grounds. At first we played on the playground, which consisted of a couple swings and a small merry-go-round apparatus. Sarah swung high in the air, comfortable in her surroundings. We just gawked at the fact that we were actually together.

> Several hours passed, and we met some of the "aunties" that take care of the kids at the orphanage. We took pictures of their room and bed. Sitting in the multi-purpose classroom/lunch room, we hugged, held, colored, and bonded. We gave Faith one fruit snack, which she savored for about 10 minutes and promptly showed off to the few children who were too young to attend school.
>
> Finally, we received a text saying we were free to leave the orphanage with the girls. The "aunties" dressed the girls in regular clothes. The girls were fitted with shoes, and rubbed with lotion. Then, we loaded in the driver's mini van and headed down the road. At once, the girls started to giggle at the feeling of riding in a van on a bumpy road. We all laughed and enjoyed the beginning of a new normal, a family of 8."

We went back to Ataco and continued to bask in the joy of our new daughters. It was so much fun to watch all of the kids play and get to know each other. Sarah and Faith would touch Cody and Isaac's red hair and pinch their white skin. They couldn't help but call us all Mzungus every now and then. They were in as much shock as the rest of us!

It was a great day, but it was short-lived. We received an unexpected call the next day saying that we needed to take Sarah and Faith back to the orphanage.

We felt so strange taking back our new kids – ones we were only just getting to know and love. In Uganda, things can change at the drop of a hat, and we knew that this might be the last time we ever saw them. There was the real possibility that we would not get to adopt them.

I can remember telling Amy that I had a peace about all of it. The peace was unexplainable, really. Here we were in a very stressful situation, and God had given me peace. We had a lot of people praying for us, and God was answering those prayers from around the world at that very moment. That is the power of prayer.

It was hard enough for us to understand what was going on, but how do you try to explain it to two little girls who can barely speak English? Faith was very upset and shaken when we left her back at Ibonde and drove away. I could tell that it was very difficult for Amy to watch her being so distressed. Sarah, on the other hand, had probably grown somewhat calloused to people leaving her. Her mom and dad died of HIV and her grandma, who they call Mukaka, had to leave them at the orphanage when she could no longer take care of them. Being old enough to fully remember these painful events in her life, she had sadly grown used to the cold reality of abandonment. We would occasionally hear her singing this song:

"Mommy come back to me,
Daddy come back to me,
This where you left me,
Life is no good."

The great news is that Mommy and Daddy did get to come back to them! Big Jesus! God answered more fervent prayers, and we got to pick them up the next day at Ibonde. It was a joyous reunion for all of us!

(Cody swinging at Ibonde)

Chapter 22

God's Blessings

The adoption agency that we went through was not prepared for a family of 8 in a 3rd world country. Finding transportation and lodging that would accommodate such a large family was difficult. Unfortunately, we were left to find most of the essentials on our own. Plans that were made in advance fell through, and we were in a bind.

We were in Fort Portal, going to court and picking up Sarah and Faith, when a missionary family who lived in Kampala, the capital city of Uganda, met us at Ataco. At that point, we were having some trouble with Ataco, and it was difficult trying to get things straightened out. That was when God blessed us with Shawn, Sarah, and their Ugandan adopted son, Jethro who came to Fort Portal on vacation. Amy had met them on her previous trip to Uganda, and we were planning on seeing them. However, we had no clue they would be in Fort Portal. They found a great place to stay and invited us to come with them. It was called Rejuna, and it actually even had hot water sometimes!

(Shawn, Sarah, and Jethro outside Ataco)

(Rejuna Guest House in Fort Portal, Uganda)

Throughout the rest of our time in Uganda, Shawn and Sarah stayed by our side. They took us to church, prayed with us, had Easter with us, floated down the Nile with us, and even let us spend a few nights at their house while we were trying to find lodging. They were very hospitable and patient, especially to such a large family.

The strange thing is that Shawn and Sarah were living out the calling God originally gave to us! Here they were, helping and loving an adoptive family in Uganda and giving them the support that they desperately needed. That was what our mission statement was! Another interesting thing is that the organization that they went through was one of the organizations that we had contacted but that never got back to us.

Wow! God's timing is perfect. Just think, we could have been in Shawn and Sarah's shoes but instead they were here helping us!

The stark reality is that we can feel alone and lost in a world that isn't our own. Just having people with us that were looking out for us and being an advocate for us lifted our spirits. They were an answered prayer, a reminder of God's love for us. He did more than just adopt us. He sent His son Jesus as an advocate for us in this world that is not our own.

Their son, Jethro, was about 4 years old and loved to play with our kids. They would beat the drums, play chase, and play toys. We often tell stories about Jethro and his straightforwardness after getting into mischief. His mom, Sarah, would say, "Hey, buddy? You knew not to do that, right?" Then Jethro would say, "Yeah. But it was fun, Mom!" We would all laugh, especially the kids.

To look back and see God's loving hands at work is amazing. We were tempted to feel like we were going through it all by ourselves, but that was never the case. God always loves and blesses His children. Shawn, Sarah, and Jethro were our blessing.

(All of us crammed inside Shawn's Land Cruiser®
returning from Fort Portal)
Photo taken by Shawn Farrell

Chapter 23

Street Kids

While we were waiting for all of the adoption paperwork and such, Shawn would take us with him on different errands and to different ministries. One of which was the "street kids" of Kampala. Here is what I write in an email back to family:

> "Yesterday, I got to go help out and minister to the street kids of Kampala. We played soccer Ugandan style. However, the road to get there was just as interesting. Shawn, the local missionary, and I caught a taxi after playing leap frog to cross the street. We were jam packed inside this taxi, and it took us 3 miles north to the slums…
>
> …a taxi in Uganda is a minivan jam packed with people. One woman was very anxious to sit next to me. I noticed her hand next to a pocket on my pants right above my knee. Her fingers slowly started reaching into my pocket. She then slung her big purse on her lap, covering her hand and my pocket. I could feel

her trying to dig into my pocket, so I grabbed her arm and started to yell, calling her a thief. I told the driver to pull over. He pulled over to a spot where he shouldn't, and a guard came out and started yelling at him to move the van as I was arguing with the woman thief. Shawn was in the back of the van oblivious to the situation and then started to climb out as the van was pulling away. The van stopped for Shawn and the guard was yelling at them to move, and Shawn finally got off the van. Crazy!

Then, Shawn told me to look beyond the valley way up high on a flat plateau type surface. I could see kids running around. He said, that was where we needed to hike to. We had to walk through the slums in order to get to the "soccer field". The slums are what you might see on TV. Nasty water and filth flowing down deep, muddy ruts in the middle of a walking path with young undressed and filthy children gazing at you as you walk by. The houses are mud huts with metal tin roofs and old clothes hanging on laundry lines. We walked by one house that had a TV blaring. Shawn later told me that these are slum "movie" theatres, and they charge 500 shillings (20 cents). Street kids go to watch to get out of the heat. They show horrible XXX movies, and they don't care what age child is watching. The Ugandans said, "Hi, how are you?" and other than gawking at two white guys walking through their neighborhood (one with a huge beard and one who is a "giant"), they pretty much left us alone…

We finally hiked up to the soccer field. I use the term "soccer field" very loosely because it is a very uneven field with ruts, sharp rocks, garbage, broken DVD's, glass, and cows along the side. The kids used one cow as a recliner and laid on it. A couple other cows had horns and didn't like to be bothered. They would charge or jab at the kids with their horns when the ball would come near. They were tethered to the ground, so they didn't go far. The kids acted like it was nothing, and they would just keep playing. They put me on one team and Shawn on the other. Not too long into the game, I hit the ball with my elbow. I guess this is a foul because they let Shawn have a free kick. He made it in, and I don't think I'll hear the end of that one. Later in the game, the ball came my way, and I kicked it pretty hard. It went far, but I missed the goal. Right after that, a bunch of kids came up to me and said that I was a giant. I don't know if it was because I kicked it hard or because they were shocked I could kick it, but I thought it was funny.

After a while, I sat down next to David. He is about 13 years old. We started talking, and David told me that his parents live in the village. He came to Kampala a couple years ago because he thought he had a job lined up. When he got

> to Kampala, he found out that there was no job, and so he was homeless with no way of making any money. I asked him if he could go back home. He said that they didn't have the money to support him. I could tell that he was opening up his heart to me, and he was sad. I told him that God is his real father. He sent His son Jesus to die for him, and that He loves him and hasn't forgot about him. David told me that he believes in Jesus. I told him that he is a lot more than a street kid to God. God loves and values him and has a plan for his life. God has not forgotten about him and to not forget about God.
>
> Other kids came up to me and wanted to jump on me or just hang on my back. They just wanted love and attention. One kid wanted to wrestle, and others wanted to just shake my hand. They don't have much, if anything. They get beaten by the police, abused by the community, and forgotten by most."

On another day at the street kid ministry, Shawn let me give part of the lesson. I got to tell them about Jesus, and a handful of boys came to Christ that day! Big Jesus! My son, Brandon, also got to come with us. The kids loved him and swarmed him like he was a celebrity.

(Brandon standing in a trash heap in the slum)

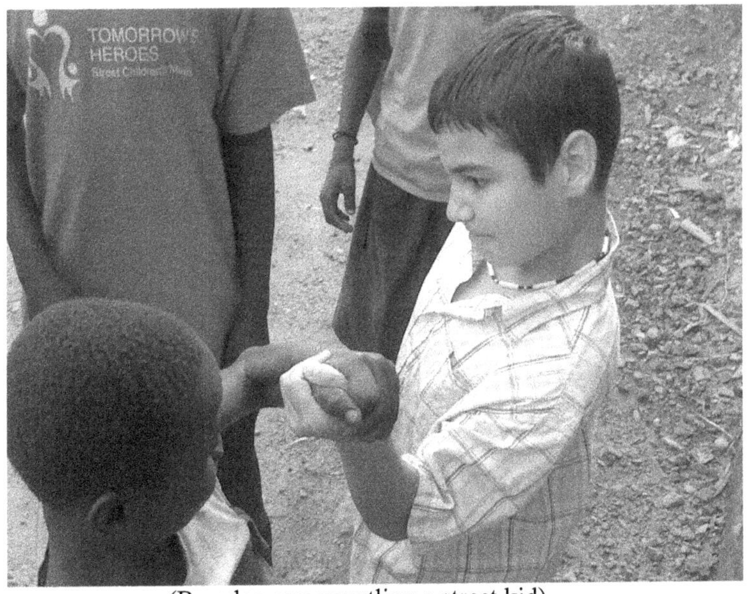

(Brandon arm wrestling a street kid)

Brandon was caught off guard at first but warmed up to them really fast. Here is what he writes:

> "Today, me and my dad went to a street kids ministry in the slum- (the very poorest place in town) when we got there I was shocked at how the people live. I mean it is pretty much a dump in some areas. A dirty creek with a bunch of garbage in it to wash clothes and bathe in.
>
> We got to where the boys were, and they wanted to play games with me, the youngest boy I saw was maybe 10 or so. The boys wanted an arm wrestling match one after another on and on, I won most of them, even with kids 13, 14, and even 15 years old. The kids and me had a blast. My dad beat just about everybody including 2 big guys together. I mean he even knocked them over, and all the boys watching cheered. I don't think I'll ever forget going to the street kids.
>
> My dad taught some of them how to get out of holds and stuff. I really enjoyed going and seeing the street kids and doing God's work."

While we were there, we had the opportunity to meet the missionaries that work with these kids on a daily basis. It was awesome to see so many Christians answering God's call to provide for the physical and spiritual needs of these "street kids."

Chapter 24

Praise's

One of the best parts about getting to be with Shawn is that he would take us with him when he went places to minister. Another place was called "Praise's." Praise was a woman who started an orphanage and school, and she needed help. Shawn would periodically take out food and other items of necessity to her. One day, Brandy, Brandon, and myself got to tag along. This is what I write:

> "One day, Shawn, Brandy, Brandon, and I went to an orphanage out in the bush. The kids swarmed the truck and literally fought each other to hold Brandy and Brandon's hands. Brandy and Brandon were completely in shock. They didn't know what to do. We went to the playground, and eventually they started chasing the kids around. The kids loved it. Whenever Brandy would sit down, all the girls would crowd around her and sit down.
>
> The orphanage has had a bad rat problem that they have been trying to correct in the past few

(The young girls at Praise's crowding Brandy in amazement)

(Brandy and Brandon inside the room where the boy had his finger chewed off by a rat)

> weeks. The kids' sores on their legs and feet won't heal properly because the rats will chew on their scabs at night. One little boy cut his hand and then went to sleep. While he was asleep, a rat chewed off his finger. This was only a few weeks ago. We saw the little boy eating with one less finger. Since then, they have been cleaning better and storing the food in plastic containers. They have seen a drastic decrease in rats."

I remember walking into a room filled with bunk beds with Brandy and Brandon. By this point, they had heard about the kid with only 9 fingers. The room was dark, musty, and very dirty. Nothing seemed out of place in the room, the beds were made, but it just felt like a rat could scurry across our feet at any second. I can remember my kids' faces like it was yesterday. They felt very uncomfortable there and were very accommodating when it was time to leave.

My mind was reeling with ideas on how to "fix" the situation. Why not buy rat traps or poison? What about sealing up around the doors? How about getting a dog or cat to chase them off? The problem was, it wasn't my problem. It actually wasn't even Shawn's problem. It was Praise's problem. That is, from what I learned, one of the hardest parts about being a missionary. I wanted to jump in and fix the problem when what I really needed to do was help them find a way to fix the problem. That is what

Shawn did. He encouraged them to find ways to get rid of the rats, and they found an effective way to do so that wasn't expensive.

I was so proud of Brandy and Brandon that day. They over came their fears and feelings of discomfort and built relationships with the kids. Watching the orphans run and play with them was one of the highlights of the trip. What a blessing from God that our kids traveled with us to Uganda to get Sarah and Faith. They learned more about God's faithfulness and Uganda's poverty than we could have ever taught them at home.

(Stool in boys' dormitory)

Chapter 25

Mukaka's House

The day we went to court to get custody of Sarah and Faith was a hot and sunny day. A courtyard was lined with a covered sidewalk and included a modest number of benches to sit on. As the morning progressed, more and more people started coming in, and pretty soon all the seats had been taken. After what seemed like an eternity, it was time for us to go to "court." This facility had actual courtrooms, but the judge elected to use his office as the courtroom for our case. Our entire family, attorney, and Sarah and Faith's relatives crammed into that little office as the judge went over the documents and fired off questions in random fashion.

Brandon accidentally sat in the attorney's seat, and the judge asked him if he was going to be an attorney some day. We all laughed and that helped to lessen the tension. The whole process inside the judge's office went by fairly quickly, and he approved us as legal guardians of Sarah and Faith! Big Jesus! This was a huge praise and an answer to many prayers. Guardianship in Uganda is as close as you can get to adoption without being in the country for 2-3 years. Finalization of the adoption would happen at a later time in the United States.

As is the custom, we took the biological family members out to eat after court. After we ate, I was anxious to get back to the hotel because it had already been a long day. However, Sarah and Faith's grandma, Mukaka (grandma in Rutooro), invited us to visit her house.

Mukaka was old and had a leathery face and big knuckles on her hands. She had the kind of rough exterior that showed that she had worked with her hands her whole life. However, she took pride in how she dressed and how she presented herself. Each time we saw her, she would come clothed in her finest attire – a brightly colored traditional Ugandan full-length dress. She could only afford one nice dress and, although it was old, she kept it in pristine condition. It was noticeable from the very beginning that she was a strong woman and that she cared deeply for Sarah and Faith.

Although it might not seem like it, it was a really big deal to be invited to Mukaka's house – especially since we were in the middle of the adoption process.

Unfortunately, adoption and corruption are viewed as one and the same in Uganda. Someone could assume that if we went to her house that we would be paying

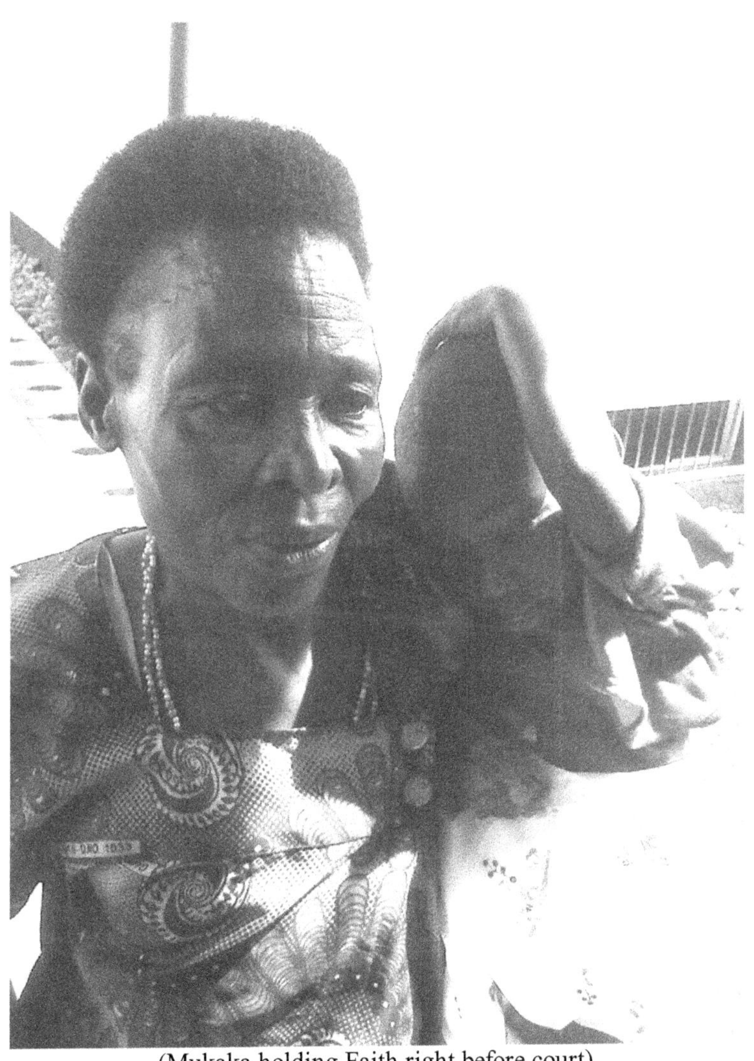

(Mukaka holding Faith right before court)

her money at the same time. This was a big risk since we hadn't gone through the US Embassy yet.

However, it really meant a lot to Mukaka. We knew that we would probably never have a chance to see where Sarah and Faith came from again, so we decided to go.

Mukaka's house was about a 30-minute drive from downtown Fort Portal. It was way out in the bush. We drove as far as we could on some really bumpy dirt and grass roads and then had to hike the rest of the way. Although it was a hot day, the path leading towards her house had many trees to give us periodic covers of shade.

While hiking, we came upon a nice house, and a lady came out to meet us. This was Mukaka's neighbor, and she was very excited to see the girls. The girls were happy to see her as well. We found out that she would often give Mukaka milk to help feed Sarah and Faith while they lived with her.

As we started to hike the rest of the way, Sarah ran way ahead of us and turned the corner. She was gone. We had no idea where she went, and we were worried about her. We sped up the pace a little bit, and the path made a turn. The trees and shrubs were thick. It was almost like walking through a tall green tunnel. Then we turned and we saw it – Mukaka's house.

(We are all hiking to Mukaka's house after court)

(Our family, Mukaka, Carol, and cousin outside Mukaka's House)

(Sarah pointing to her mom's grave, a time that was undoubtedly etched into her memory)

Mukaka's house was made of mud and sticks and had a tin roof. It was small and had a dirt floor. Their wasn't much furniture in it, and the kitchen was a fire pit inside of a mud stick shack in the back yard. There was a wide shallow hole to the side of the house where they probably got the mud to make the house. Surrounded by banana trees, there was no other house in sight. The smell of smoke filled the air. It was a very simple and modest house to say the least.

As soon as we saw the house, we found Sarah walking out of it with an old plastic cup filled with water, and she had a piece of sugar cane in her mouth. Sarah was at her grandma's house, and she felt at home.

It wasn't long before neighbors started showing up to see what all the excitement was about. Not every day were Mzungus walking around out in the African bush. Mukaka was very excited to tell them that we were adopting Sarah and Faith. She was even more excited, however, to tell them that we had adopted Brandy and Brandon when they were little. This was something that we hadn't planned on. The fact that our kids were with us gave Mukaka a peace about our family. She was able to see for herself and show others that we had previously adopted. Our kids were healthy and doing well. This was extremely important to her.

Mukaka was thrilled to show us all around her house. She took us to the grave where Sarah and Faith's mom was buried, which was about 30 feet in front of her house inside the covering of trees. She then took us inside the house. I could barely fit through the front door since I am so tall. The living room was completely packed, and we were standing in a circle.

It is amazing to think that in her small simple house, Mukaka poured out so much love for her children and grandkids. Placing them for adoption wasn't easy for her. Most likely, this was one of the most difficult decisions she had ever had to make. This was noticeably evident at a later date when I write:

> "…I noticed Sarah and Faith looking very intently at their Mukaka (grandma). Then I noticed that she was wiping away tears from her eyes. This was very hard for her to do. To give her grandkids to strangers, just hoping that they would have a better life and be well taken care of..."

As we all stood there, inside the small living room, Mukaka wanted to pray for us. She then started to pray and to praise Jesus in the most touching way! She lifted her hands and with her face towards heaven, started praising Him and jumping up and down. Mukaka was praising God because He was taking care of her granddaughters and had undoubtedly answered her prayers.

Here was a poor elderly woman who had lost most of her children to AIDS and had done all she could do for her grandchildren. She sold almost all of her land, little by little, to provide for them. Then, when there was nothing left, she took Sarah and Faith to an orphanage. She would visit them, but deep down she knew that this wasn't the best answer. She gave of herself until there wasn't anything left to give. And then she entrusted to us two of her most valuable possessions, Sarah and Faith, and jumped and praised God at the same time!

Her heart was aching knowing she might never see them again, but at the same time it was filled with joy because she knew that God hadn't forgotten about her and her grandkids! Mukaka is a living testimony of perseverance and remarkable faith – faith that could only come from a real relationship with Jesus!

Throughout the past few years, our struggle was wrestling with God on what He wanted us to do and where He wanted us to go. It was a struggle that led us to a humble woman who gave everything she had to give. And this woman, without anything to brag about in terms of material things, had more of a home than most could ever dream of in this world. I can only hope that our home, in the ways that matter the most, will always remind our kids of Mukaka's house.

www.ingramcontent.com/pod-product-compliance
Lightning Source LLC
Chambersburg PA
CBHW060509030426
42337CB00015B/1817
9780692401910